How to Get Beyond Loneliness

LARRY YEAGLEY

REVIEW AND HERALD® PUBLISHING ASSOCIATION
HAGERSTOWN, MD 21740

The author assumes full responsibility for the accuracy of all facts
and quotations as cited in this book.

Scripture quotations identified CEV are from the Contemporary
English Version. Copyright © American Bible Society 1991, 1995.
Used by permission.

This book was
Edited by Gerald Wheeler
Copyedited by Jocelyn Fay and James Cavil
Designed by Helcio Deslandes
Cover photo by PhotoDisc
Typeset: 11/13 Palatino

PRINTED IN U.S.A.

02 01 00 99 98   5 4 3 2 1

R&H Cataloging Service
Yeagley, Lawrence Robert, 1933-
    How to get beyond loneliness.

    1. Loneliness.   I. Title.

                155.92

ISBN 0-8280-1294-6

CONTENTS

INTRODUCTION

I awakened at 5:00 a.m., pulled on my jeans and sweatshirt, slipped my feet into my walking shoes, and quietly tiptoed out of the vacation cabin in Bar Harbor, Maine. The dense fog rolling in from the ocean created an eerie environment for my morning walk. Just as I approached a historic courthouse I noticed a cemetery nestled between huge white pines. Large drops of dew dripped from the needles onto the slender tombstones now covered with green moss.

I knelt down by one stone after another to read the epitaphs. Quickly I discovered that most of the early settlers bade farewell to this life at a young age. Diseases that are no longer a threat, thanks to modern medicine, had cut down infants and young adults.

Modern medicine may have reduced measles and whooping cough, but it hasn't snuffed out one of the greatest risk factors in premature deaths from all causes. Loneliness is still on a rampage in highly mobile and hard-driving America.

My son took a photojournalism class at the university. He chose to depict loneliness in America. I suggested that he walk the large campus of a nearby Veterans Administration hospital with a camera in hand. The despairing loneliness engraved on the faces and bodies of the people he captured on film stunned me.

I met one of those veterans when he was admitted to the hospital where I worked. It was Allen's fourth admission for severe dehydration and uncontrolled diabetes. He lived alone in a tiny house trailer and had no family in town. People in nearby trailers never visited him.

After the doctors had stabilized Allen, I pulled a chair up to the head of his bed. "Will you be having any visitors while you're here?" I asked.

"Afraid not," he said quietly. "You see, I don't have a friend in this world. They say I was nearly dead when I came in here. Good thing I dialed for help when I did."

"Isn't there *anyone* who knows you?" I said in disbelief.

"No, sir. I'm telling you the truth. I had the phone put in, hoping that maybe someone would call a wrong number and for a few moments I'd think that someone was thinking about me. It never rings."

I looked at his dehydrated face. A few tears ran from the outside corner of one eye and coursed down the deep creases in his face. He stopped speaking. I think it was too painful.

When I assured Allen that I would visit him every day, he smiled and mouthed a thank-you. I left his room, convinced that I had just spoken to the loneliest man in the world.

The world is full of lonely Allens, but they don't all live alone. Some are married and emotionally isolated. I met Girard when I visited him in his home.

His wife believed that because Jesus is coming back soon, she needed to shun all frivolity. Frivolity in her book included romantic conversation, physical touching, and sexual contact. She insisted on separate bedrooms and spoke to Girard only to call him to meals. Her husband sank into a lonely state. He was a stranger in his own home.

Children can be lonely. Arlene convinced me of that.

"My mother died when I was 8. I remember how frightened I was. I felt as though I'd be alone the rest of my life.

Introduction

Putting me in the car, my father drove me to an aunt's house. He hugged me and told me he'd be back for me in two days. Then I watched him drive away. I still feel that heavy weight in my heart." She paused to regain her composure.

"Two days later I waited by the kitchen window for him. All day I sat there until it was bedtime. Days turned into weeks. My father never returned. To this day I don't know his whereabouts."

"What has gone on inside you since that time?" I asked.

"I have always felt robbed of my childhood, and I've been very, very lonely. My husband is a good man. I love him. My girl does everything she can to help me, but inside something is still missing."

I often think about Arlene. Picturing that desperately lonely 8-year-old girl, I know that she was still inside Arlene when she died of cancer at 55.

Shelly lived with her parents, but loneliness turned to hopelessness that led to her suicide attempt. I met her in the intensive-care unit. She was happy that the doctors had saved her life, and so was I. A bright girl, Shelly had a smile that quickly won my heart.

Her doctor released her to the care of her parents, but he insisted that Shelly receive counseling. However, her parents had no insurance and no money for counselors. Since I was the hospital chaplain, the doctor asked me to see her.

Shelly tested me every day she came to my office. She'd wear unmatched shoes, braid one side of her hair and not the other, chew bubble gum obnoxiously, attach long rows of huge safety pins to her skirt, or paint her face excessively. I passed her tests by complimenting her and by suggesting other bizarre ways of dressing.

The girl told me she hadn't wanted to kill herself. She'd simply wanted to force her parents to spend time with her. When they didn't heed her urgings, she acted out of desperation.

Customarily she'd wake up in the morning after her parents had already left for work. Eating breakfast alone, she packed her own school lunch. At 3:00 in the afternoon the bus dropped her off a block from her home. Then she changed clothes and fixed supper in time for her father's arrival home. He ate in front of the TV. Shelly ate alone in the kitchen. All attempts at talking to her father failed. Her mother usually picked up fast food on her way to her second job.

At Christmastime the girl's mother announced that she was taking a weekend job as a salesperson in a clothing store. As the woman left the house on that first weekend, Shelly tearfully begged her mother to stay home with her, but her mother left without acknowledging her daughter's sadness. That's when Shelly took the pills.

After one counseling session I called her parents and insisted on seeing them. Firm and confrontive, I intended to jolt them with the seriousness of their lifestyle. To my amazement, they had no idea that Shelly was lonely.

Shelly and I visited together for three months. I wanted to become her friend so she'd be comfortable contacting me if the home scene didn't improve. As a reward for her commitment to the counseling process I gave her a $10 gift certificate from a popular ice-cream parlor. She promised to treat her school friends on Saturday night.

Shelly, Girard, Arlene, and Allen are just four of the many lonely people I have met in my nearly four decades of working in human services. Loneliness seems to have become an epidemic during that time, but I discovered that few people seemed alarmed about it.

Some early religious authors stated that the cure for loneliness is having a relationship with God. One author even viewed loneliness as a gift from God. I tested such ideas during my encounters with lonely people, but they didn't harmonize with reality. I came to know devout Christians who were lonely. So there had to be more to the loneliness equation.

People often recommend volunteering as a way to prevent loneliness. I worked with volunteers in hospitals and hospices. Many of them were lonely. They dreaded going home after their stint of duty. Although busy, they were still lonely. Filling life with doing good was not a panacea.

Sometimes people equate being alone with loneliness, but I met a man who contentedly lives in his cave home. He feels secure in his seclusion, not lonely.

I decided to explore the riddle of loneliness when I was attending a national conference of chaplains in San Diego, California. The association of hospital chaplains to which I belonged insisted that I stay in the expensive hotel where the proceedings would take place. They made no attempt to encourage room-sharing.

During the first meeting the moderators encouraged the chaplains to "share their journey" with their colleagues. As I listened to stories of growth and job satisfaction I became extremely uneasy, because my journey had come to a roadblock at the death of my son. I shuffled to an empty room that night with a heavy heart.

The next morning I went to the hotel restaurant, only to discover that breakfast would cost almost as much as my daily meal allowance. I walked for nearly two hours in search of a fast-food restaurant, but the fancy hotel district forbade yellow arches high in the sky. Not finding anything, I slowly climbed the stairs to my room and drank hot chocolate provided by the hotel.

In the afternoon I attended a seminar on loneliness, hoping to receive a lift from the painful feelings inside me. The presenter reviewed a book I had already read. Its simple answer to lonely people was *Trust in God and you won't be lonely*. That didn't seem right. Having committed my life to Christ as a boy, I thought I had a relationship with God.

Leaving the seminar, I walked to a nearby shopping mall. There I watched the people, wanting to see if anyone looked as miserable as I felt, but all the shoppers were in a rush. Returning to the empty hotel room, I drank two more cups of hot chocolate.

On Sunday morning I heard a friendly voice calling my

name and turned to see my good friend Rex Edwards. He had found an inexpensive motel and the inconspicuous yellow arches at the edge of the hotel district. I climbed into his rental car. Soon we were enjoying a meal and enriching conversation. Little did Rex realize that his hospitality was touching and soothing the pain of loneliness that had taken a heavy toll on my soul.

Loneliness can lead to something positive. Once I attended a meeting in the Catskill Mountains of New York. It had convened to elect church leaders, but business came to a standstill as everyone argued about how many people from each ethnic group would be named to the nominating committee. I had high expectations for my church, but reality was far different. A sense of isolation came over me as I walked through the woods to an empty summer cottage where I'd sleep. The silence of that cottage was deafening. I was cold, lonely, and heartsick.

Pulling a pad of paper from my briefcase, I crawled under the covers and began writing about the backpacking trip my sons and I had taken that summer. The ideas flowed smoothly, and I wrote faster than usual. Finishing the story, I edited it several times. When I returned home, I sent it to a publisher. It was my first published story.

My first two weeks in a boarding school produced a loneliness that made it difficult to study. Restless, I felt trembly all over and constantly fought back burning tears. Gradually I developed new friendships that distracted me from my sorrow over leaving home.

I've concluded that curbing the epidemic of loneliness doesn't rest on simplistic formulas and quick fixes. The complexity of loneliness demands more than glib answers.

CHAPTER ONE

Society's Contribution

Loneliness doesn't mean you are weak, ill, or lacking in faith. You don't need to approach it by first probing for personal failure. Constant introspection about personal deficiencies could actually deepen loneliness. That's why I'm skeptical of some things I read.

For example, Dan Kiley recommends a practical inner faith for lessening or eliminating loneliness. He says that faith "compels you to believe that you have special powers inside of you. This faith says that only you can truly heal your loneliness. All the answers to all your problems lie within you" (*Living Together, Feeling Alone*, p. 11).

Kiley is placing the responsibility and the solution for loneliness squarely on the shoulders of the lonely person. I differ with him. You don't yell to a drowning nonswimmer, "Go for it—you have it within you to make it to shore." Neither do you tell someone floundering in loneliness, "The power within you will pull you through. Just use your practical inner faith."

If all the answers to all of your problems lie within you, there is no reason for faith in a power greater than yourself.

Kiley treats lonely people with a self-reliance program, because he believes lonely people are too dependent on others.

No wonder lonely people are embarrassed to admit personal loneliness.

I was excited when I read what Carin Rubenstein and Phillip Shaver wrote: "If thirty-five million Americans are lonely each month, the causes cannot come only from within each person; something must be wrong with society itself. We don't have to look far to see some of the causes: widespread mobility; a high divorce rate; impersonal, crime-ridden cities; the substitution of television and home videotape viewing for face-to-face community life; bureaucratic procedures and letter-writing computers that increasingly take the place of personal business transactions. . . . Loneliness reminds us that social forces, not individual shortcomings, are the ultimate cause of widespread loneliness" (*In Search of Intimacy*, pp. 3-14).

We do need to address some causes of loneliness related to personal qualities and deficits, but first I would like to cite a few causes that result from society itself.

UPROOTEDNESS

I conducted grief support groups for six years in Battle Creek, Michigan. Many corporate executives attended. Lonely people who had been uprooted by their companies (sometimes twice in a year), they felt disconnected from important relationships. Others reeled with confusion after death in the family. None of them were weak people. Loneliness caused by the death had become complicated by loneliness that followed frequent moves over which they had little control. Their uprootedness resulted from the need to survive.

I noticed that some families were more resilient than others. If they had relatives living within a reasonable distance, they adjusted to losses quite readily. Those transferred to Battle Creek from a greater distance usually struggled with the upheaval of the move.

Charles William Stewart talks in his *Minister as Family Counselor* about four kinds of families. The *overly rooted* family is inflexible, making it almost impossible for a person to stray far from the family of origin. The *well-rooted* family allows autonomous movement within family togetherness. The *thinly rooted* family consists of people who move frequently from the family of origin. They put down tentative roots with intentions of returning to the family again. The *uprooted* family produces the nomads of American society. They leave the family of origin and maintain no serious connections with it.

The thinly rooted families and the uprooted families will most likely experience loneliness. Many of the people in my support groups came from the latter two types of families. In most cases they did not choose their style of rootedness.

FACELESS VOICES

Technology has contributed to the depersonalization in our world. If you doubt this, try calling your phone company. Be prepared to be swallowed by the computer jungle that I encountered.

Computerized Voice: Thank you for calling. If you know the extension of the party you are calling, enter it now. If you are inquiring about your account, press 1. If you wish to open an account, press 2. If you need service, press 3.

I pressed 3.

Computerized Voice: Thank you for calling. All our service representatives are busy at the moment. Many problems can be solved without speaking to a service representative. Please press 1 and enter your area code and seven-digit number now.

I did exactly what the faceless voice commanded. Then the jungle deepened.

Computerized Voice: If you are unable to receive incoming calls, press 2. If you are unable to make outgoing calls, press 3. If you are unable to complete long-distance calls, contact your long-distance carrier. If you need further assistance, please stay on the line for the next available operator.

The computerized voice didn't mention my problem of squeaky noises during long-distance calls. I was puzzled. Just as my arm became numb, the voice gave a final message.

Computerized Voice: If you wish to make another call, please hang up and dial your number. Goodbye.

I put the phone down. No way would I subject myself to

that twice in the same day.

Our computer-generated communication age is faceless and flat. The warmth of a friendly voice and an accepting smile has virtually disappeared from some enterprises.

Les Carter, Paul Meier, and Frank Minirth observed, "With our many sophisticated capabilities the individual seems to take a back seat to computers" (*Why Be Lonely?* p. 53).

A computer buff friend of mine tells me that computers will soon do all business transactions. Personal contact with a merchant will be an experience of the past. If this prediction comes to pass, loneliness could be more prevalent than it already is.

My mother made most of the bread for our family. Her flour supply came from an old mill in White Oak, Pennsylvania. My father threw two bushels of wheat into the trunk of the old 1939 Pontiac. My sisters and I piled into the back seat. Off we went to see Pappy Greenley. Pappy met us at the loading dock. He and my father carted the two bags of wheat to the big hopper. The grinder swallowed the wheat, and the fresh flour poured into clean white bags.

After we loaded the sacks of flour into the trunk, Pappy ushered the whole family into his cluttered office. He took payment, and Pappy and my father exchanged news and humor. Pappy's little rat terrier was the center of excitement. The old man leaned back on his creaky swivel chair, pushed his broad-brimmed hat off his bald head, and yelled for Skippy to catch the fleas on his head. Skippy jumped on Pappy's shoulders and nibbled at the old man's scalp. We giggled with delight.

Just before we left, Pappy pretended to be serious. "Now, I don't suppose the Yeagley children like candy. Well, that's too bad. I was thinking about filling this bag with penny candy. Oh well, maybe I'll just fill the bag in case I'm wrong." Then the long-bearded Mennonite miller filled a large bag with licorice straps, root beer barrels, Tootsie Rolls, Hershey's Kisses, Kits, lollipops, and other favorites. As he handed the bag to one of us, my father reminded us to say thank you. In spite of our eagerness to devour the candy, we expressed our gratitude.

Pappy was more than a flour merchant—he was our friend. He was part of the family. A shopping trip was an adventure. Chewing candy all the way home, we laughed and talked about Pappy and Skippy for days afterward. What a contrast to computerized shopping.

ISOLATION

I began chaplaincy training in Worcester, Massachusetts, in the days when sick people stayed in hospitals until they were well enough to return to their homes. Physicians decided who would be hospitalized, not insurance companies. That's why Mary was in Room 312.

She greeted me warmly. "Pull up a chair. I need to talk to a chaplain," she instructed me. Despite the construction noises rising from outside the medical ward, she held me in conversation for nearly an hour.

After the visit I hurried to the nurse station to read Mary's chart. The hospital was treating her for several conditions, one of them severe anemia. As I read the chart the head nurse peeked over my shoulder to see whose chart I had. She had noticed my long visit.

"Oh, you poor chaplain. Mary captured you," she laughed. "Mary lives all by herself in a third-floor flat. She's totally isolated. No family. No friends. She comes to the hospital over holidays. We always know a holiday is approaching when Mary appears. We're the only family she has."

Isolation had locked Mary into a state of loneliness. She had little motivation to cook, so she nibbled on junk foods. Half of the time she went to bed hungry. Eventually she would be hospitalized with a variety of ailments.

Mary's isolation became all too familiar to me. Visiting hundreds of the three-story tenements in Worcester similar to the one in which she lived, I felt the loneliness. Many of the residents were physically unable to go shopping. Their human contacts consisted of the delivery person and an occasional caseworker.

Children experience isolation when their parents divorce, when a parent dies, and when they are too different from their peers. Also, children become easy targets for their peers' cruelty. Paul Tournier talks in *Escape From Loneliness* about the emotional isolation of children who are teased in school or in the home. He believes this can cause loneliness that follows the child into adulthood.

I identified with Tournier's observation, because I developed a nervous tic just as I was about to enter elementary school. I'd open my mouth wide until my eyes were as wide as saucers dozens of times in a few seconds. I knew it was happening, but I couldn't stop it.

My siblings and my schoolmates teased me unrelentingly. They gave me nicknames to match my facial contortions. No adults came to my rescue. I found myself surrounded by ridicule. Loneliness engulfed me.

One day I asked my mother, "Is there anything I can do to keep from making funny faces?"

She took me to see Dr. Heisey, the family doctor, who brushed it off casually. "Don't worry about it. He'll grow out of it."

The emotional isolation caused by that tic was the source of my private loneliness.

Tournier also speaks about the emotional isolation of children who live with abusive parents. He believes the loneliness caused by such isolation has long-term effects.

I've noticed loneliness in the lives of clergy. They experience isolation from parishioners who expect superhuman feats of sacrificial service. The demands made on their time isolate them from their families. I am not alone in this observation.

Herbert Benson described the clergypersons he met at a conference he attended in New York City: "By and large, these religious leaders, representing a variety of denominations and creeds, had this in common: they were overworked and underpaid, their jobs were very stressful, and they often had no one to turn to for their own counseling or support" (*Timeless Healing*, p. 162).

I attended a church conference in Indianapolis, Indiana, decades ago. Meeting a new friend who seemed depressed, I invited him to walk around the city and have lunch with me. We found a little café where people didn't seem in a hurry to leave. Eating slowly, we lingered for at least an hour. He told me of his plans to take early retirement from the hospital where he ministered. His superiors considered his style of patient visitation antiquated, and he felt rejected and lonely.

Together we discussed various options that would allow him to use his strengths to avoid isolation and loneliness. Later he told me that our luncheon was the highlight of the conference, because someone had listened to him. He had not spent his time alone without someone to affirm him.

David Myers noted in his *Pursuit of Happiness* that Americans are spending more time alone. They marry later, divorce more often, and live more of their lives independently. This amounts to increased social and emotional isolation. Society views self-reliance and independence as virtues, yet such lifestyles encourage loneliness.

I live near a large Amish community that has avoided the problem of self-reliance. One of my neighbors has a bakery next to her house. She sells her baked goods along the highway. Her Amish neighbor sells her pies for her at a farmers' market. My next-door neighbor harvested his wheat. Three wagons, three teams, and 12 men hauled the sheaves of grain to the separator. When my neighbor and his family went to a funeral in another state, an Amish friend milked his 28 cows for four days.

I stopped by the Amish school to give a message to a friend. Inside the school I found a dozen mothers scrubbing the floor and laughing together. They were preparing for the opening of school.

One Sunday I drove by the Amish bishop's home. Nearly two dozen children jumped on a trampoline while the parents visited inside. I didn't see a single child hanging in the background. All were engaged in the fun.

I discovered that all the families know and help each other. They seem to have counteracted the isolation that plagues many Americans. I wish other segments of American society could learn from the Amish.

As I reminisce about some of the lonely people I met in psychiatric wards, I have to agree with Henri Nouwen, who said: "Isolation is among the worst of human sufferings" (*The Wounded Healer*, p. 60).

Competition

A competitive spirit that has infiltrated shop, office, school, and even the church has riddled our society. Competition isolates. It doesn't draw people together. Constant vying with others turns potential friends and confidants into foes.

I try to combat competition on the highway. At a four-way stop I relax and motion the other driver to proceed. At that moment the highly competitive driver of the Intrepid behind me blasts his horn. He passes me at his earliest opportunity. I often wonder if the Intrepid driver and I could have rewarding dialogue if stripped of our metal and fiberglass cages. Could we eliminate the crippling isolation, given the chance to make eye contact?

Our society encourages competitive individualism. It demands a high price. Painful loneliness can result, for instance, from the anxiety and tension created by competition in the educational environment.

Competition-induced loneliness was apparent on the ballfield when I taught elementary school. Two athletic sixth graders picked up sides. The best players always got chosen first. When the sides were filled, the rejected boys and girls would sheepishly vanish to the merry-go-round and the swings.

After a few days of watching the lonely children wandering around the playground, I made new rules. The selection would continue until all the children were chosen. Team captainship would rotate, giving every child a chance. When less-experienced batters stepped to the plate, the pitcher would pitch slower and give away hits. Home runs would not be counted. Players would receive tips for improving their skills.

The plan worked. When less-athletic captains chose players, they frequently chose less-athletic children earlier in the pickup. Students began complimenting each other. They gave me tips for improving my own swing. I felt that we had reduced the competition and the loneliness.

Divorce

Divorce is often one of the loneliest experiences. It produces loneliness for both parents and children, yet people treat it so lightly. When I lecture on the topic of loss, frequently a person from a divorced family will tearfully describe the deep loneliness that comes as a result of divorce.

Our society has used the media to eliminate the word *commitment* from relationships. All that seems to matter is self-pleasure. This has taken many people to divorce court and through the hell of loneliness.

People from broken homes often attend the support groups I conduct. Rejection and loneliness are the most frequently reported feelings at such sessions.

Archibald Hart in his book *Children and Divorce* tells about the divorce of his parents when he was 12. Thirty-seven years later he felt that he had received only second best. He believes that divorce produces loneliness that can be acute and long remembered and advocates saving an existing marriage if at all possible.

Counteracting Trends

A young couple told me how they were planning to counteract the trends that had produced loneliness in their home. They would reduce television viewing drastically, thus allowing time for family fun and communication. The wife decided to view mothering as a significant career. She would seriously pursue her college degree after the children were older, providing quality time and quantity time with her family now. The husband decided to seek help for his addiction to work. Retiring at 45 would no longer be his goal. He wanted time for intimacy with his wife and children. As a family they would simplify life and pause to smell the roses.

I affirmed them, assuring them that society has no right to enslave us in a lifestyle that produces loneliness. They challenged the societal trends that eat away at the relationships meant to meet our basic human needs.

You have a right to confront a society that robs you of wholeness, community, and intimacy. If loneliness is sapping your strength, look outside of yourself before you search for reasons within.

CHAPTER TWO

Definitions

My visit to the island of Sulawesi in Indonesia was enhanced by the hospitality of the islanders. Early one morning two church leaders took my wife and me for a daylong tour of the island. As we rode in the Jeep station wagon they pointed out all the important features of the landscape. They told us of ancient customs and modern innovations. We ventured into dark caves dug by Indonesians under the cruel force of the Japanese during World War II. We viewed a volcano from a distance, then walked around the campus of a mission school while the youngest guide told us how he had climbed the coconut trees during his student days at the school. By noon we reached the headquarters of the mission territory. Our hosts invited us to be seated in the simply furnished conference room. A few minutes later brightly dressed women carried trays of cool drink and tasty sweet breads. One woman passed a bowl of water and a towel so we could wash our hands before eating. We were hungry. The food was satisfying. We were grateful for their generosity.

Two hours later we arrived in the town where the older guide lived. He happily announced that his wife had prepared a few refreshments for us. We entered his tidy home, but soon discovered that his wife's hospitality was far from simple. A lace cloth covered her dining room table. Her best dishes and silverware were neatly arranged. The food came in courses. We were impressed with their generosity, but we were not very hungry. I ate until I was stuffed.

Back in the station wagon our hosts announced that the people of Sulawesi had invited us to a banquet in our honor. It would begin in an hour at the home of the president of Mount Klabat College. Although overwhelmed by the hospitality of the people, hunger was the furthest thing from our minds. We returned to our guest room, freshened up, and walked across the campus, hoping that their last meal of the day was a light one. It wasn't so. I had never seen such a huge table filled with so much good food.

In an effort to be polite, I took small portions and ate slowly. I complimented the people freely on the delicious food, hoping they would not notice my poor appetite. The host kept urging me to have more. The Indonesian people on Sulawesi eat slowly and enjoy their food. This saved the day for me. During the two hours of the banquet I was able to sample most of the delicacies on the table.

Carin Rubenstein and Phillip Shaver liken loneliness to hunger. "Loneliness warns us that important psychological needs are going unmet. Loneliness is a healthy hunger for intimacy and community—a natural sign that we are lacking companionship, closeness, and a meaningful place in the world. Mild hunger enhances life and makes eating all the more rewarding. Mild or occasional loneliness is also life-enhancing. It causes us to acknowledge our separateness and appreciate our deep need for other people" (In Search of Intimacy, p. 3).

My wife's uncle, Forrest Pratt, visited our home. He sat in the living room with our four boys gathered around him and told them stories of his years in a Japanese prison camp, where he was fed a starvation diet. His large frame wasted away and disease took its toll. The boys had never known such inhumane treatment. They were hungry at least three times a day, but their hunger was satisfied regularly. None of them could imagine the hunger that Uncle Forrest described.

According to Rubenstein and Shaver, "severe hunger, in famine proportions, is a very different matter; it is a sign of societal failure. And so is widespread loneliness" (*ibid.*).

Whether or not loneliness is healthy depends on the degree of loneliness and whether or not the needs pointed out by loneliness get met adequately. There is a difference between hunger and starvation, just as there is a difference between transient loneliness and chronic loneliness.

The hunger definition of loneliness makes sense to me. It helps me to be more comfortable with my occasional loneliness. And when I meet people who are always lonely, I can be more understanding of their agony.

It has fascinated me how people of different disciplines define loneliness. The definitions vary with their perception of loneliness and their academic training. I will share a few examples.

I have read almost all of Henri Nouwen's books. I've also heard him lecture. Often I get the feeling that he struggles with personal loneliness, though I admire him for his vulnerability and honesty. He says, "Loneliness is one of the most universal human experiences, but our contemporary Western society has heightened the awareness of our loneliness to an unusual degree" (*Reaching Out*, p. 14).

Les Carter, Paul Meier, and Frank Minirth approach loneliness from a psychological and spiritual point of view. They say it is "a sign that things are not perfect in our world. We should remember that it is also a normal response to nonfulfillment of emotional and social needs. . . . Loneliness is a state of feeling that one is not accepted or does not belong. It implies varying degrees of emotional pain, an empty feeling, a yearning to be with someone, a restlessness" (*Why Be Lonely?* pp. 49-74).

Lowell Ditzen gives a rather scholarly definition. He says that loneliness is an "acute, chronic, nondirected sense of aloneness that breaks down man's integration" (*You Are Never Alone*, p. 45).

Charles Durham in his *When You Are Feeling Lonely* regards loneliness as a signal to us that we have a relationship deficit, that something's missing and we need to take some kind of action to remedy it.

Letitia Anne Peplau and Daniel Perlman, in the most complete study of loneliness that I have read (*Loneliness—A Sourcebook of Current Theory, Research, and Therapy*), suggest that loneliness is how we respond when we don't have sufficient social reinforcements. It is a response to some specific kind of relationship deficiency. Loneliness is the result of a perceived or real discrepancy between what a person hopes for in interpersonal relationships and what one is actually experiencing. It is a feeling that someone is missing.

David Myers puts definition and causes together when he says, "Lacking opportunities for self-disclosure—for sharing our likes and dislikes, our proud and shameful moments, our worries and dreams, our joys and sorrows—we are painfully lonely. Loneliness isn't being alone. That's solitude. It's feeling alone" (*The Pursuit of Happiness*, p. 151).

William Hulme puts it this way: "Loneliness is psychic pain—a dread in the depths of one's being. Its origin is in the separateness of our uniqueness and the alienation that may ensue. Perhaps at times you felt so different from others that you experienced virtually no contact with them" (*Creative Loneliness*, pp. 23, 24).

Bruce Fisher, a divorce therapist, has an interesting definition of loneliness: "Loneliness can be a vacuum or an iceberg. Lonely people need to deal with the vacuum inside by sucking up everyone around in order to fill their void. Or they need to deal with the iceberg inside by trying to gain warmth from everyone around" (*Rebuilding*, p. 37).

These definitions, written by professional people, suggest that loneliness is multifaceted. The definitions given to me by participants in bereavement support groups show the same thing.

"It's a bit like a nostalgia, a searching."

"I'm alone in my apartment, and I feel the need to talk with someone. No one calls. I feel lonely. When there is nobody home when I call on the phone, then it is hard to lift the loneliness."

"When I feel weak, vulnerable, and depressed and I need someone to sound my feelings off of, I feel lonely when nobody is there."

"Disconnected. Isolated. Not cared about. People are afraid of me."

"A very low feeling with no energy or emotion. A feeling of being somewhat lost. A feeling of disconnectedness with my husband."

"Only someone who has lost a mate can know this empty feeling. I miss the companionship, the loving, and knowing someone loves me in return. We did everything together, and now I feel I'm only half a person."

"Thinking sad thoughts. A house that is too quiet."

"An empty feeling. A physical pain in the chest. No future. Numb."

"I feel deserted and desolate."

"When I am lonely, I feel a deep need of companionship. If no one is around to meet this need, I will go find something to eat."

Some definitions of loneliness cannot be tucked into one sentence. Melanie described it to a group of 26 people in a support group: "My husband stayed with me long enough to get me pregnant. When my body shape changed, he vanished in search of pretty girls. I gave birth to my little girl who is now 5. For the past five years I have been alone and deprived of adult intimacy. Don't get me wrong. I love my little girl, but relating to a child is not the same as having an adult confidant. I do pretty well much of the time, but there are intense occasions when I long for someone to touch me. To touch me, just so I know I'm real, all right, and valuable."

Melanie told the group that she often yearns to be back in her mother's arms. We encouraged her to visit her mother, who lived a few hours away. "Ask your mother to hold you in her lap and hug you the way she did when you were a child," I suggested. She took the trip and enjoyed her mother's touch of tenderness.

Your Turn

Now it's your turn to define loneliness. It will necessitate understanding the causes of your loneliness. Keep a journal. Define it in a few sentences. Define it in your life story. Resist the common urge to rationalize and minimize your loneliness. Admitting loneliness takes honesty and courage. Understanding your loneliness is the first step in turning a crippling experience into a growing one.

CHAPTER THREE

Breaking the Alienation

The first human family didn't experience loneliness. They lived in a perfect home environment. Domestic violence was nonexistent, and they enjoyed the flawless beauty of flowers and trees. God visited with them every day and expanded their spiritual understanding. Each day ended with fulfillment and peace of mind.

But it all changed when Adam and Eve made the self-centered decision to do as they pleased. Fear gripped them, and they hid themselves. Open dialogue with God ceased. Talking with God would never be the same. *Alienation from God* created a core loneliness that will nag at the human family until Eden is restored.

Their self-focus tainted the intimacy between Adam and Eve. Blaming spoiled their trust. Distrust and selfishness flowed into their offspring. *Alienation from each other* led to the first funeral. From that day onward no family has been exempt from broken relationships.

Alienation from self led to confused thinking and feeling. Their self-centered course blinded Adam and Eve to the purpose for their existence. Disloyalty to God destroyed their innocence. The fullness of joy that comes from being in rhythm with the heartbeat of the Creator diminished.

God's perfect creation became a hostile environment. Forced to leave their homestead, Adam and Eve had to battle with thorny plants and plant field crops each year in their struggle to keep food on the table. Taking natural resources for granted, they created pollution. Instead of caring for the earth, the human family abused it.

Alienation from God had a domino effect. Alienation from others, self, and nature followed in quick succession. Humanity had drawn the blueprint for loneliness.

GOD'S REACTION

Les Carter, Paul Meier, and Frank Minirth have commented that "God's response to the loneliness of humanity is not to back away from us, but to become more deeply involved in redeeming us from our human condition" *(Why Be Lonely?* p. 65).

Love is not easily thwarted. When Adam and Eve closed the door to evening strolls with God, He immediately attempted to communicate with them in other ways. He took their self-inflicted loneliness seriously, knowing how much their survival depended on His love. God would not give up on His new creation.

I can appreciate God's predicament to a fraction of a degree. After I'd been courting my wife for a year, one of her former boyfriends showed up for her graduation. She became unsure of our relationship and asked for time to think it over. Did I give up? Never. I immediately thought of new ways to woo her more effectively.

We can trace God's response to Adam and Eve's decision to take the path of loneliness in the book of Genesis. He found ways of maintaining closeness with them, even though those ways would plant His own feet on the path of loneliness.

The Gospels more fully spell out God's reaction. He sent His Son, Jesus, to identify with guilty sinners and with innocent sufferers. David Seamands points out that the Healer of our hurts is also the Feeler of our hurts. The One who wipes our tears also weeps with us. The Lifter of the lonely nearly died of loneliness in the Garden of Gethsemane. He knows, cares, and understands how we feel (*If Only*, pp. 57-67).

Some religionists paint a distorted picture of God. They distance Him from the lonely. Instead of alleviating loneliness, they increase it. But studying God's reaction to human loneliness does the opposite. Jesus' life is the supreme chapter in God's reaction to our loneliness. His death on the cross draws us close to Him. The more we study that chapter, the more loneliness loses its death-grip on us.

Henri Nouwen said, "I am afraid that in a few decades the Church will be accused of having failed its most basic task: to offer men creative ways to communicate with the source of human life" (*The Wounded Healer*, p. 38).

Even more basic is the responsibility of the church to show people how God communicates with them. It's an enormous task. The church can attempt to enumerate God's avenues of communication, but love that is not easily thwarted has innumerable ways of breaking down alienation. Ways that the church has not thought of yet. Our God is too big to define.

MENDING THE BREAK WITH GOD

I am indebted to Nouwen for his rich insights into the far-reaching effects of intimacy with God.

"The more you learn to love God, the more you learn to know and cherish yourself. Self-knowledge and self-love are the fruit of knowing and loving God. Laying our hearts totally open to God leads to a love of ourselves that enables us to give wholehearted love to our fellow human beings" (*Letters to Marc About Jesus*, p. 75).

"The closer we come to the heart of the One who loves us with an unconditional love, the closer we come to each other in the solidarity of a redeemed humanity" (*Lifesigns*, p. 51).

"The man who prays not only discovers himself and God, but in the same meeting he discovers who his neighbor is" (*With Open Hands*, p. 102).

"When we know ourselves to be deeply anchored in that divine covenant, we can build homes together. Only then can our limited and broken love reflect the unlimited and unbroken love of God. We can only stay together when the staying power comes from the One who comes to us to stay" (*Lifesigns,* p. 42).

Nouwen's comments confirm a conviction that I have had for many years. An openness with God produces a strong sense of purpose and meaning. God's purpose becomes a reality because knowing God opens the way for an appreciation of self, others, and the universe around us. Friendship with God connects us with something and Someone much more expansive than self. We see the unfathomable meaning of life of which we are a part. Despairing loneliness cannot thrive indefinitely in the presence of such a friendship.

Wayne Oates said, "The awareness of the presence of God provides a sense of companionship and turns loneliness into solitude" (*Nurturing Silence in a Noisy Heart,* p. 28). Solitude, as we shall learn later, is positive and an antidote for loneliness.

The companionship that Oates speaks about is not stiff and highly structured. Nor is it what some religious writers recommend. Jesus came to show us that God is our friend. When we come into the presence of our friend we relax and tell Him exactly what is on our mind. We don't have to weigh each word, because our friend already knows our motives and understands, accepting us as we are. In fact, He comes to us first. And He is interested in giving us peace, not condemnation.

William Hulme wrote, "The inner dialog with God and the outer dialog with people support each other" (*Creative Loneliness,* p. 78). "When our relationship with God occupies our inner space, the security coming from our dialog with him enables us to accept the natural limits to outer dialog. Then our relationships with others are constructive" (*ibid.,* p. 72).

Hulme does not believe that a relationship with God is the total answer to loneliness. He recognizes that we need people, but without God in the life we simply use people for our own purposes. That is destructive and results in greater loneliness.

I meet young people who engage in sick relationships because they are lonely. When I suggest that they consider a relationship with God, they laugh and wave me off.

David Myers in his *Pursuit of Happiness* points out that young people who don't take a relationship with God seriously, and don't care to be a part of a large and abiding family, find little meaning in life, and hence are more lonely.

I conducted spirituality groups for young women in eating disorders programs. Their lives were broken. Loneliness was eating away their hopes for happiness. I took them outdoors to enjoy the sunlight, sky, trees, and flowers and encouraged them to contemplate the goodness of God. Gradually some of them saw that they were children of God, cherished by their Creator. Accepting God as their friend helped them to confront their own weaknesses without guilt and loneliness.

Seamands believes that Americans have adopted a blame game that pins all their pain on others. He suggests that we assume responsibility for alleviating our brokenness instead of singing the "if only" song.

We can take the initiative by turning to God in worship, praise, and thanksgiving. As we bow before our Creator in adoration, His power will be released into our life and give us the ability to see ourselves as precious children of God. Receiving the courage and the desire to reach out to others in relationship, we will be reminded of His re-creative power in the natural world He has made.

Instead of praying, *Lord, if only I weren't so lonely, I could enjoy life,* we will break the alienation by praying, *Lord, if only I open my life to Your warm embrace, my loneliness will not be so crippling. Help me to open my life to Your presence.*

It was never God's intention that human beings should meet all their needs only in relationship with Him. After He created Adam, God looked at all the animals and birds with others of their kind. He concluded that it is not good for man to live alone, so He made Eve as a complement to Adam. God created us as social creatures. Apart from others we cannot be complete. To ignore that fact, to encourage others to satisfy their need for relationships with God only, is to try to destroy what God made us.

God designed our relationship with Him in such a way

that social relationships would be desired and enhanced through intimacy with Him. That's why a relationship with God is not the total answer to loneliness. He created us with a need for fellowship with others.

Mending the Break With Others

Derek Kidner speaks to the origin of broken relationships: "Companionship is presented in Eden as a primary human need, which God proceeded to meet by creating not Adam's duplicate but his opposite and complement, and by uniting the two, male and female, in perfect personal harmony.

"The shattering of the harmony of man and wife, not by any mutual disagreement but by their agreeing together against God, proved at once how dependent it had been on His unseen participation. Without Him, love would henceforth be imperfect, and marriage would gravitate towards the sub-personal relationship foreshadowed in the terms *desire* and *rule*" (*Genesis,* pp. 35, 36).

Before the first family agreed to turn against God, human companionship enabled them to experience love so completely that loneliness did not exist. After the journey of self-centeredness began, the man God created equal with the woman ruled over the woman. His partner now became his chattel. He ruled her instead of loving her as an equal.

It was the beginning of loneliness in the home. That loneliness reigns in homes today, ripping marriages apart, devastating children, gnawing at the fabric of society.

A nationally conducted seminar has been popular among conservative Christian groups during the past two decades. The key idea is that the man has absolute authority in the home. He is the ruler. Some of my friends have bought into this concept that is so contrary to the Genesis model. A number of them have lost their marriages. Others are still together, but loneliness lurks in their homes.

It seems ironic that a Christian organization would promote a theory so opposed to God's ideal for human relationships. Is it possible that women's rights are trampled in the name of religion? Can the humanly made chain of command rip the heart out of family intimacy? Alienation from others is bound to result from this false idea. Deep loneliness will surely be a by-product, and it will obliterate God's plan for human relationships.

Mother Teresa has said, "As far as I am concerned, the greatest suffering is to feel alone, unwanted, unloved. The greatest suffering is also having no one, forgetting what an intimate, truly human relationship is, not knowing what it means to be loved, not having a family or friends" (*Mother Teresa*, p. 91).

Mother Teresa's words accurately describe how many women feel when treated less than equally. I have had more than my share of pastoral visits with women who live with churchgoing men who espouse the ruler theory. Should not the church champion the Genesis model of human relationships? Isn't it time for the church to break the alienation that exists in many marriages and homes?

Another idea that has gained favor is that *I can be just as good a Christian without ever going to a church building.* I hasten to tell people who try to live by this idea that Bible baptism is baptism into the body of Christ. That body is Christ's church. We are baptized into the fellowship of believers.

Hulme emphasizes that "only through human associations can people develop their potential to relate to nature, to themselves, and even to God—as human beings. It is not coincidental that religious practices tend to be communal" (*Creative Loneliness*, p. 76).

Myers, in his *Pursuit of Happiness*, points out that intimate attachments are the vital center of a person's life from the cradle to the grave. That includes, among other areas of life, the church.

In his book *Loneliness and Spiritual Growth* Samuel M. Natale maintains that friendship is an important factor in loneliness. Quality relationships are critical in staving off loneliness. In our quest for quality relationships we should include every part of our community.

During World War II my family lived on a farm in

Cornwall, Pennsylvania, that was bordered on one side by the Cornwall Railroad. Bethlehem Steel Company transported iron ore from the mines to the smelter on that railroad line. The company installed a huge Fairbanks scale along the tracks opposite our barn and erected a roomy building over it. Bill Quarry was the scalemaster.

What could have been a lonely existence on the farm turned into a lively association with a generous soul. Bill assigned me the role of car-counter and number-recorder. On a pad of paper I recorded the numbers of cars as they slowly crossed the scale. I carried fresh ice water to the scale house for Bill and the train crews. When Bill had no trains to weigh, he told me wild stories that delighted my childhood imagination.

When the train schedule allowed, Bill came over to our farmhouse. He played "Repaz Band" on our piano while we kids danced around the living room. When one of us was ill, Bill checked in to make sure we had enough medicine and food. Often he shared his ration stamps with us so my mother could buy extra staple foods. Bill was a friend who knew how to listen to the woes and the joys of the entire family.

Quarry had a heart for the unfortunate children of his little town of Rexmont. He often asked my parents if the young people could spend time on our farm. Some of the children were my age. This expanded my circle of friends just when I needed close friends with whom I could share my boyhood dreams.

One of my Rexmont friends was mentally challenged. Although Ray was the target of pranks, he never seemed to be offended. His big smile seldom disappeared. I liked Ray very much. We could talk about everything that really mattered to us. He never criticized me, and I never ridiculed him for his slowness.

Nouwen described our type of friendship: "An intimate relationship between people not only asks for mutual openness but also for mutual respectful protection of each other's uniqueness" (*Reaching Out*, p. 20).

Mending broken ties with others occurs when we have a

genuine interest in them. That does not come naturally. It is a gift that God gives us when we have a close relationship with Him. The apostle John said, "If we believe that Jesus is truly Christ, we are God's children. Everyone who loves the Father will also love his children. If we love and obey God, we know that we will love his children" (1 John 5:1, 2, CEV).

According to Seamands, mending such brokenness has an extra bonus. "By opening ourselves to one another, we always open ourselves to God in new and greater ways" (*If Only*, p. 147).

MENDING THE BREAK WITH SELF

As I met a staff psychiatrist at the hospital elevator one day, he surprised me by his offhanded comment: "Larry, I've been thinking a lot lately about self-actualization. I have come to the conclusion that it is nothing but selfishness." Boarding the down elevator, he was gone before I could respond.

My thoughts went back a few years to my experience with an encounter group in Boston. The philosophy behind my group stated that I am the most important person. If I think something is OK for me, it *is* OK.

Since the days in that encounter group I have met people who have been disciples of selfism. Self has been the main focus of their life. They have used relationships as a means of reaching their own desired ends. Friends were disposable. But when life dealt them unmerciful blows, they had no supportive relationships. Loneliness plagued them.

A distorted view of self results from not having a close relationship with God. But knowing Him helps us realize how He evaluates our worth. Knowing how God views us gives us hope, not a sense of despair. And knowing God brings an appreciation of servanthood so that we no longer use relationships to gain our own desires.

Scripture says that all of us have sinned and come short of the glory of God. That seems like a bleak picture if we stop there. But God didn't stop there. He looked at the family who chose the path to loneliness and saw them through the eyes of possibility. The Lord evaluated them on the basis of what His redemptive grace could accomplish.

I learned a lesson in placing a proper value on myself in Waterbury, Connecticut, when I became the pastor of a small congregation that worshiped in rented quarters for 40 years. Shortly after I arrived, Jim and Harry Rice found a vacant church. Its former congregation had begun to build a new building, but ran out of money. They capped the basement and rented it to the Head Start program. The parsonage was livable, and the parish hall was large enough for our congregation, but it was in total disrepair.

Jim and Harry took me into the parish hall. My face fell. I said, "Gentlemen, I don't see how you can turn this building into a church."

Sitting me down on a pile of scrap lumber, they pulled a piece of paper out and began to draw a diagram. One of them said, "Pastor, you have to look at this building through the eyes of possibility. We're accustomed to doing that, because we have remodeled buildings before. Now take a look at what we plan to do."

I studied the sketch carefully and asked lots of questions. Eventually I began looking at the old parish hall through the eyes of possibility. Rubbing shoulders with Jim and Harry helped me to look at the building in terms of what lots of hard work could do. When we fellowship with Jesus every day, we look at ourselves differently. We see a person redeemed at a great price, one who fits into God's eternal plan to give unspeakable joy to every individual who will be open to His grace. Viewing ourselves through God's eyes, we witness someone whom God will use to bring hope to the hopeless. God is making a masterpiece out of what would otherwise appear to us as worthless raw material.

In church I sing a song with the little children. The words go something like this: "Brown and Yellow, Black and White, all are precious in His sight. Jesus loves the little children of the world."

One Sabbath we were singing that song, and a little girl on

the front row started shaking her head no. I told that little child that the more she learns about Jesus, the more she will understand how special she is to Him. I often think about her. I hope she values herself the way God does. Low self-esteem is a major part of loneliness. It can begin in childhood. I pray that I was able to change the way she viewed herself.

An appreciation of the valuable person you are is indispensable in preventing loneliness. As Anais Nin wrote in her diary: "The lack of intimacy with one's self, and consequently with others, is what created the loneliest and most alienated people in the world" (quoted in Robert Blair Kaiser, "The Way of the Journal," *Psychology Today*, March 1981).

MENDING THE BREAK WITH NATURE

Speaking of the human family, John White said, "From this lofty position of supremacy man sinned and fell. In that fall he was both morally and mortally wounded. Sin had warped his personality. But it had done more. It had alienated him from God and distorted his relationship with creation. He now had to earn his food by painful toil" *(Putting the Soul Back in Psychology,* p. 23).

I believe that God is eager to cooperate with us in mending our distorted relationship with creation.

When is the last time you walked barefoot in a freshly dug garden and felt the dirt squeezing up between your toes? How long has it been since you wandered through tall dew-covered meadows in the early morning to watch deer? Did you ever lie down on your back and imagine that the billowing clouds resembled elephants or whales?

If you can remember only walking on sidewalks, blacktop parking lots, or carpeted floors, you may need to mend your break with nature. Mending your break with God is an excellent way to be reunited with His matchless creation.

Hulme suggests that estrangement from the creation of God has brought loneliness. When we are alienated from the natural world, we become estranged from our own human nature. Contact with nature is helpful, because the Creator of the natural world is also the Creator of people. The same precision and care went into designing both. When we recognize that fact, we feel like we are part of a master plan.

Intimacy with the natural world reveals God to us, if only in a limited way, and enhances our relationship with Him. Another dimension of God's purpose for us becomes clear, and despairing loneliness grows more remote.

My son David and I slipped his canoe into Bass Lake, near Traverse City, Michigan. Five minutes into the trip the rain began to fall, but we had come prepared. Pulling on our slickers, we paddled as cheerfully as we would have on a sunny day. We were seeing Michigan through fog and rain, an experience that has probably escaped most vacationers. God was cleansing that part of His big world right in front of our eyes. At the end of the trip I realized that God had cleansed me too.

James B. Irwin went to the moon in *Apollo 15* in 1971. Later he wrote about that experience: "What really moved me and touched my soul was that I could feel God's presence there. . . . I actually looked up to see the earth. That beautiful, warm, living object looked so fragile, so delicate, that if you touched it with a finger it would crumble and fall apart. Seeing this has to change a man, has to make a man appreciate the creation of God and the love of God" (*To Rule the Night*, p. 60).

My soul was moved and touched during a speaking tour in British Columbia for the Hospice Association of British Columbia. On Sunday the treasurer of that organization took my son and me on a hike in Wells Gray Park. As we walked toward Helmchen Falls, Frank would stop and tell us curious facts about a plant or a flower. Then he'd say, "What a design. There has to be a Designer." Frank's appreciation of nature drew the three of us closer to God.

IS IT JUST A THEORY?

For at least 10 years I have been contemplating the idea that our alienation from God, others, self, and nature is producing our loneliness. At times I felt that perhaps it was just a theory, yet I had my theory confirmed by my many contacts with extremely lonely people. When I lectured on the topic of loneliness, I shared the theory. Many people sat up and listened carefully. They identified with what I was saying.

Imagine my delight when I read *Why Be Lonely?* by Les Carter, Paul Meier, and Frank Minirth and discovered that they see separation from God, separation from others, and displeasure with self as factors in loneliness.

The delight was complete when I read *Creative Loneliness* and found Hulme adding the fourth factor—inability to relate to nature.

I am convinced that loneliness dissipates when we make serious attempts to break the alienation with God, others, self, and nature. I believe that the first step is reestablishing a rewarding friendship with God. When we increase our understanding of His character, we topple the other three alienations. The result is less loneliness and a more satisfying life.

CHAPTER FOUR

Community and Intimacy

New York City frightened me. I stepped up to the courtesy booth at the airport and inquired about a hotel. The young woman behind the counter made temporary reservations for me. She wrote directions so I could find my way. Nervously I walked to a bus stop. There a woman in her eighties greeted me.

"Is this your first time in New York?" she asked.

"The first time on my own. Sure is big, all right," I answered.

"It's really a friendly city," she added. "Where are you staying?"

"Here's the name of the place." I showed her the paper bearing the name and directions.

"Why are you staying in a fancy hotel? That's a waste of good money. I always stay in the Y. Cheaper and friendlier. You come with me, and I'll show you where the Y is, and you'll thank your lucky stars you did."

I discovered that she owned a tea plantation in Argentina. Her last visit to New York had been eight years earlier, but she knew all the subway stops. I followed her to the street level, down three blocks, and over one. "See that stone building on the right hand side of the street? That's the Y. Good luck, young man. And next time don't bother with those fancy hotels."

For $5 I had a tiny room with no bath. It was steamy hot. I opened a window, but the huge building next to the Y cut off the air. Quickly bathing in the communal shower down the hall, I dressed for supper. Down the street I found a little restaurant. Sitting at the counter, I ordered soup and a sandwich. The cook/owner couldn't understand my accent. "Speak up, buddy. I ain't got all day," he yelled. Finally he served me. I ate quickly, then left.

In the morning I walked to the train station. All the pedestrians looked straight ahead. The only person who made eye contact with me was a panhandler. When I refused to give him money, he quickly left, muttering unkind things. New York City didn't seem friendly to me. I felt lonely.

Years later I was riding in a bus with my friend Peter. We were leaving Denver to visit in the country. "Larry, I get sad when I leave the city," he said. "Los Angeles is my home. I grew up there. I feel secure with the noises and the people. I have a lonely feeling just now as we leave the city."

"But, Peter," I protested, "how can you not enjoy the quiet of the country?"

"Larry, Los Angeles is where my community exists. Life pulsates in the city. I don't know everybody in the city. All the people are simply background against which my friends and I live. I will never leave the city."

Peter taught me that the city doesn't produce loneliness. The lack of a close and familiar community can cause it, though.

My father was a sharecropper for a wealthy landowner in Bethesda, Maryland. The landlord's son came to spend the summer on the farm. The chauffeur drove him to the farm, carried his suitcases to the front porch, and promptly returned to Bethesda. Young Lawrence spent the first few weeks in deep loneliness. Slowly my community became his, and the loneliness disappeared.

We went fishing with Harry Boyer. Sunny days by the creek in the meadow drew us together. Bill Quarry, the scalemaster, thrilled us with his far-fetched stories. The Watkins man came to the farm in a horsedrawn buggy. He spread his

41

ointments and liniments on the kitchen table. Every week he had a special treat for us kids. The Jewel Tea man made summer fun, because tasty drinks or candies topped his weekly visit. The Gearharts' Bakery truck stopped twice a week. Mr. Yorty, the driver, pulled out long drawers filled with stuffed doughnuts, cookies, and eclairs. Samples were always forthcoming. The scrap man was our source of spending money. We gathered old metal and sold it for the war effort in the early 1940s. Lawrence, the city slicker, soon discovered that we farmers had a community even though we didn't live in the center of a bustling metropolis.

Community is different for each person. Some require a larger community than others. A community with people of various ages and backgrounds stimulates one person, but limiting community to peers may be more satisfying to another. All of us require a community of reliable and helpful people. We need relationships and a network of acquaintances. And we must be open to others, to take social risks. For all of us, community needs to be people who stay with us in times of success and failure. Community is a solid base for human existence. Without it we are lonely.

My dictionary defines *commune* in this way: To exchange thoughts and feelings; to be in accord or agreement. The word *community* refers to a group having common interests, likeness, or identity.

For five years I taught elementary school. During the first year I went to the mandatory teachers' convention. It dashed my hopes of being part of a community. Those attending displayed their best bulletin boards and their spectacular units on social studies. Teacher after teacher told success stories and major breakthroughs with difficult children. Not a soul talked about failure and discouragement. Although I had both problems, I received no opportunity to air them. There seemed to be an orchestrated attempt to hide thoughts and feelings about failure. I left feeling totally disconnected from the rest.

Most of the conferences I attend for clergy have a similar ring. Ministers relate exciting stories of conversions and church growth. Experts offer their foolproof plans for every-thing from marriage counseling to conflict management. Polished pulpiteers present models of exegetical preaching. Stories of church construction and fund-raising make the process sound so simple. But no one speaks about the raw heartache and recurring urges to enter a different profession.

Where is the community? "By the honest recognition and confession of our human sameness we can participate in the care of God who came, not to the powerful but the powerless, not to be different but the same, not to take our pain away but to share it," Henri Nouwen answers. "Through this participation we can open our hearts to each other and form a new community" (*Out of Solitude*, p. 43).

A genuine community embraces people of many back-grounds. It is not threatened by the expression of pain, neither is it tricked into believing that the community will weaken when anyone expresses failure. We can expose the pendulum swing of life in community with no fear of rejection or reprisal. A community of this nature is a treasure worth keeping.

We can lose community by moving, since it forces us to leave a total community behind. If you have a choice in the move, adjusting to loss of community is easier. Visiting the new area and becoming acquainted with the new community prior to leaving makes the move less traumatic.

Three trips to Michigan preceded my transfer from Texas. I looked at housing, set up a bank account, contacted the util-ity companies, visited the shopping malls, subscribed to the local newspaper, went to the library, consulted with the cham-ber of commerce, and talked with as many residents as I could. When the moving van finally pulled into town, I felt that I had part of my community in place.

Divorce can dissolve a community quickly. Former couple friends feel awkward relating to you in the same manner. Invitations drastically diminish. Your church community may not accept you as warmly as they once did. Change in your economic status may force you to spend long hours in the workplace. Your place of residence may shift. Suddenly you find yourself thrown into the world of the singles, whether you like it or not. Such a new world can be threatening and full of loneliness.

Mourning loss by divorce is essential and healthy, but those who have successfully adjusted have shared an important secret. Don't yield to the temptation of playing the "if only" game. Learn from your past mistakes quickly, then look ahead. Plan to do something constructive with the rest of your life. This is not the trite advice of people who have never divorced, but that of divorced people who have successfully confronted loneliness.

Loss by death fractures the family system. It takes time for the family to reconfigure itself. Until that happens, the survivors experience a major loss of community. Much assimilation and accommodation take place before the family is again in a reasonably functioning state. Within any family some individuals struggle with separation anxiety, making family grief more complex.

Experts now recognize that loss of community acts as a major factor in the breakdown of the family after such loss. I highly recommend support groups and individual counseling. They can ease the adjustment and prevent unnecessary and chronic loneliness.

When our expectations of our community are unrealistic, our disappointment can be deep enough to produce severe loneliness. I have met this in my work as a pastor. People join a church community with some strong and impossible expectations, then become lonely when their hopes shatter. A current trend has families choosing a church that provides services for them. The ideas of servanthood and discipleship are not in vogue, although the church has historically been a service organization, one of people of faith reaching out beyond the walls of the church building. But now when a church does not meet personal needs, loneliness can prompt members to leave.

Don't misunderstand me. Church is a fellowship—the fellowship of the broken. The church is also a community for restoration, but reaching out beyond the fellowship of the church itself is a vital ingredient in the healing of loneliness within the church. The building of community is an ongoing process. If you acquire new friends every year and attempt to strengthen existing friendships, your community will be large enough to meet many of your personal needs.

A new friend of mine is extremely lonely, with no community. For six years she cared for her sick husband single-handedly. His care was so demanding that she had no time to nurture friendships. By the time he died, she was bereft of both husband and community. Also extremely tired, she has had no energy to develop a new community. I am visiting with her, allowing her to do her grieving, and trying to be a little part of her new community. Hopefully she will be able to rebuild her community and use that community as a base for developing intimacy.

Carin Rubenstein and Phillip Shaver emphatically state: "The only lasting remedies for loneliness are mutual affection and participation in a genuine community" (*In Search of Intimacy*, p. 18). We cannot settle for less.

INTIMACY

When they hear the word *intimacy*, some people think of sexual intercourse. I met a man who thought he could alleviate his loneliness after his wife's death by visiting a house of prostitution. His increased sexual activity did not diminish his loneliness. In fact, he thought it intensified it. I told him that sexual activity is not necessarily intimacy. If it were, meeting the need for intimacy would be quite simple.

Rubenstein and Shaver have observed that "intimacy for hire is like cheap fast food; one leaves you nauseous or still hungry, the other, lonely and emotionally empty" (*ibid.*, p. 3).

Perhaps a trip to the dictionary will help. The adjective *intimate* means marked by close association, acquaintance, or familiarity; belonging to or characterizing one's deepest nature; marked by privacy and informality.

Nouwen obviously grasped this meaning when he said,

"We probably have wondered in our many lonesome moments if there is one corner in this competitive, demanding world where it is safe to be relaxed, to expose ourselves to someone else, and to give unconditionally. It might be very small and hidden. But if this corner exists, it calls for a search through the complexities of our human relationships in order to find it" (*Intimacy*, p. 23).

The Elixir of Life

I have felt nudged to write about loneliness ever since I read James Lynch's words in 1977: "From the quiet comforting of a dying person to the cuddling of an infant—in our earliest years, in adulthood, whether single, widowed, divorced, or married, whether neurotic, schizophrenic, or normal, whether human or animal—one factor unites us all, and that is dialogue. Dialogue is the essential element of every social interaction, it is the elixir of life. The wasting away of children, the broken hearts of adults, the proportionately higher death rates of single, widowed, and divorced individuals—common to all these situations, I believe, is a breakdown in dialogue. The elixir of life somehow dries up, and without it people begin to wither away and die. Those who lose it as children, adolescents, or adults feel acutely what they have lost and struggle to get it back" (*The Broken Heart*, p. 215).

Lynch says that dialogue is more than love. Requiring a response from another living human, it is sharing of joy, pleasure, displeasure, irritation, fatigue, and anger. "It consists of reciprocal communication between two or more living creatures. It involves the sharing of thoughts, physical sensations, ideas, ideals, hopes, and feelings. In sum, dialogue involves the reciprocal sharing of any and all life experiences. An individual may lack a dialogue of love and still remain relatively healthy as long as other forms of human dialogue are maintained and the individual does not become socially isolated" (*ibid.*, p. 217).

His research brought him to the conclusion that lack of dialogue—loneliness—is the greatest risk factor in premature death from all causes. He chastises a government that spends a fortune on research into the role of diet and exercise in preventing premature death while not spending a penny on investigating the effects of loneliness on health.

His study of the populations of Nevada and Utah uncovered shocking facts. Premature death rates in Nevada soared above those of Utah. The rates closely correlated with the family stability in Utah and the instability of family life in Nevada.

Instability in the family breeds loneliness, because dialogue gradually diminishes and finally disappears, leaving family members without the elixir of life. They are relationally bankrupt, and their human needs go unmet.

What are the essential human needs? I have asked that question of many people in my bereavement support groups and eating disorders groups. Their list is not complete, though. You can probably add a few of your own.

Giving and receiving love.

A sense of belonging.

Being needed.

Trust.

Protection.

All levels of intimacy.

Food, clothing, and shelter.

A sense of purpose.

A feeling that you make a difference.

Laughter.

Unconditional acceptance.

Security.

When you have dialogue with one person or preferably several people, you will more fully have such needs met. Loneliness is not likely to be a persistent visitor.

If you have only one close friend and lose that individual, loneliness can become a problem. It is healthier to have several intimate friends so that the loss of one of them doesn't leave you completely devoid of dialogue.

Dialogue is a process that begins spontaneously and develops over a long period of time. It is largely nonverbal, a mutual response between two persons. They can sense when dialogue is occurring without speaking a word. James Lynch says it is giving the most sublime gift to another person—the gift of ourselves.

Infidelity in marriage is not something that can be kept secret, because it disturbs nonverbal dialogue, alerting the other spouse that something has changed. A sense of isolation and loneliness develops, but the partners don't walk away from the marriage until dialogue sinks below what Lynch calls a certain critical threshold.

He observes that "divorce is a major life-threatening event. The central threat is to the individual's very existence, his humanity. In divorce the individual is rejected and left to feel like a profound failure. Life is dialogue, and in divorce that idea crashes over the individual like a tidal wave. It is a major threat to life, as is readily verified in health statistics" (*ibid.*, p. 226).

Dialogue is the result of heart-to-heart communion. No *thing* can ever serve as an adequate substitute. Gifts of sports cars, clothes, houses, and jewelry can't replace it. Travel and months at a lavish resort are hollow and dissatisfying when heart does not speak to heart.

The search for intimacy that doesn't find dialogue is a vain one. My work in alcohol rehab units proved that to me. The patients bought into the myth that alcohol would help them socialize and have plenty of friends, but alcohol didn't give them true intimacy. It loosened their tongues and lowered their inhibitions, but provided no heart-to-heart dialogue.

William Hulme summarizes the false claims for alcohol: "Alcohol produces within us sensations we would experience through intimacy with other people. The addict feels 'high' or 'good' or 'relaxed.' People in bars often appear to be very sociable, yet an acquaintance of mine who frequents bars describes them as 'dens of loneliness.' The need for chemical stimulation to facilitate sociability indicates that at least some of the sociability is superficial" (*Creative Loneliness*, p. 17).

Human beings have an innate need for intimacy, but it does not come by promiscuity, alcohol, or other drugs. We find it when we are just as willing to give intimacy as we are to receive it.

My culture did not endow me with the ease of giving and receiving closeness. I wanted to be close, but I was afraid. When I tried to be close, I was awkward about self-disclosure. My awkwardness set me up for failure. Fortunately I had some extremely patient peers who helped me to understand the dynamics of intimacy.

Since my days of trial and error, I have found many good books written on intimacy and directed at various age groups. Some authors have even analyzed the physical distance required for building relationships. Wayne Oates speaks of measuring intimate space. Six to 18 inches is the distance of lovemaking and comforting. A couple stand one and a half to two and a half feet apart in public. Four to seven feet is the sphere for business and social gathering. Twelve to 25 feet or more is the public distance. The closest distance requires a mere whisper for communication, but the farthest distance demands careful enunciation and louder speech with gesturing—perhaps even an amplification system (*The Psychology of Religion*, p. 151).

Distance and nonverbal dialogue are not the only factors in gaining the elixir of life. It may well go back to how our parents spoke to us.

On June 4, 1996, I heard a report on National Public Radio about research on how parents talk to boys and girls. The researchers examined the influence of nature and nurture on how emotionally rich children are.

They found that the nervous systems of baby girls are more developed than those of infant boys. Baby girls make more eye contact with parents. They have longer attention spans than boys and make more noises. The study observed that parents imitated baby girl noises more than baby boy noises. They engaged in more feeling talk with infant girls. Parents entered into goal-oriented conversations with little boys and emotion/feeling-oriented conversation with little girls.

Two toys were given to the children, a toy store and a take-apart car. Girls usually played with the store, while boys chose the car. Parents had emotion-rich conversations with the girls, but their conversations with the boys were more task-related.

Adults spent more time talking about what had happened in the past when they were with the girls. The girls talked more elaborately about past experiences than the boys did. Girls spoke about sadness more than the boys. Expression of emotions was more acceptable for girls than for boys.

The researchers felt that the sharp difference in psychosocial conversation had a direct bearing on the ability of the children to form close relationships. It may well be that a boy's lack of ability to carry on emotionally rich conversation may negatively influence his ability to form meaningful relationships. Emotional isolation could result from his stronger task-oriented way of life.

Parents need to pay close attention to the nurturing of male and female children, because early childhood could be the formation time of loneliness.

MY BROTHER'S KEEPER?

A young man from Arizona regularly shopped at a Wal-Mart store. Just about every time he noticed a disheveled old man sipping a cup of coffee in the snack area. After weeks of observation he realized that not a single person spoke to the man—in fact, they went out of their way to avoid him.

"That's when I decided to change the old man's world," he said later. "I pulled a chair up next to his and wished him good morning."

The man looked up in surprise and said, "You're the first person who has said good morning to me in years."

After a long conversation, the shopper turned to the old man and said, "I've got to go now, but I want to shake your hand."

Happily the man offered his hand, saying, "I can't remember the last time I shook hands with anyone."

Now the two men meet at Wal-Mart every week. They eat breakfast together and swap stories. The old man has revealed his alcohol problem. The younger man prays with his new friend. He has offered to tell him about Jesus' power to deliver him from alcohol and loneliness. I suspect that the old man will accept the offer as the trust level deepens.

Here is a person who had no community and no intimacy. Shunned by others, he could easily have fallen through the cracks and died friendless, but the younger man believes in being his brother's keeper.

We need to discover ways of overcoming personal loneliness, but assuming responsibility for others must increase if we are going to stem the tide of loneliness in America. Western society has overstated individualism and self-sufficiency to the point that they have created a relationship vacuum.

I challenge you to break the barriers. Speak to people when you shop, fly in a plane, go to an auction, wait for the walk light at a crosswalk, stand in line at a checkout, or go to church.

The next time you enter an elevator, have some fun. Instead of watching the floor numbers, greet the occupants. You'll shock them, but they'll be relieved to have the silence broken. Those people are a part of your new community. Get acquainted.

Here's a guarantee: if you become your brother's or sister's keeper, you'll break through your own loneliness. Your potential for building community and intimacy will increase exponentially.

CHAPTER FIVE

Creative Solitude

A balance between work, relationships with others, time alone, and communion with God will foster good mental health. *Balance* is the key. If you spend most of your time working, relationships will suffer. But if you are always around people, you will have little time to yourself for personal and spiritual development. The chances of becoming lonely increase when we lose such balance.

Some people avoid being alone at all costs. The thought of solitude terrifies them. They consciously plan to be around people and sounds at all times. Radio and TV personalities become family to them. Talk radio is popular because it helps them avoid solitude. Computers have now become a convenient way to prevent solitude. Lonely people afraid of solitude talk via computer into the early-morning hours.

Avoiding solitude exacerbates loneliness instead of preventing it. Many of the lonely people I know flee solitude because they view it as negative. They believe that solitude will carry them to the depths of permanent despair.

I'd like to suggest that solitude can indeed be detrimental if you do not balance it with work, relationships, and communion with God. We must approach solitude intentionally. It needs to be creative. Creative solitude is a vital part of preventing chronic and despairing loneliness. I have personal experience to support this concept.

I was 14 years old when I began high school by correspondence. For two years I cared for my father's small farm during the day and studied at night. During the day my parents worked two jobs to meet the mortgage payment, leaving me alone for at least 10 hours at a time.

At first I feared being alone. There wasn't another soul with whom I could share my thoughts. House and barn were empty of persons, but full of sounds I'd never noticed before. Focusing on work was extremely difficult. I jumped from one task to another, never completing any of them. Or I walked aimlessly about the farm, longing for my father's car to appear in the lane.

I knew I had to develop a different perspective on being alone. Gradually solitude became a creative force in my life.

First I asked my father to give me a work assignment each day. This brought structure into my solitude. When my parents came home I received their affirmation and praise for my diligence. Solitude was a chance to achieve a goal.

On rainy or snowy days I spent hours in the shop. I dismantled wooden fruit boxes and built knickknack shelves for my mother's collectibles. My biology course required me to become familiar with the trees, flowers, grasses, birds, and mammals in my area, so I roamed the quiet fields and forests in search of specimens.

On sunny mornings I quickly finished the chores so I could sit on a grassy bank and play my harmonica. The notes floated into the open air and left me feeling in touch with God's big world.

Sitting on the harrow or the cultivator behind Bob and Prince, our two draft horses, allowed me to think about what I wanted to do in life. It enabled me to refine my values and my goals. Dreams developed. My resolve to be a minister strengthened during such creative solitude.

In my solitude I learned skills, planned my future, studied God's handiwork, and audibly talked to God. Eventually I cherished my solitude. Now I enjoy it and view it as an antidote for loneliness.

Creative solitude prepares me for fellowship with my family and friends, enhances my relationship with God, opens my eyes to my own potential, and gives me a deeper appreciation for the natural wonders of creation. In addition, it has provided me space to grow. In quietness my meditation strengthens my friendship with God. I discover my value as a person, not because of what I am doing, but by recognizing who I am.

When I spend time alone, I am refreshed and energized to reach out to others. I have a new desire to mingle with people, whether they be friends or strangers. Solitude gives me the incentive to develop my community. I have a desire to be an intimacy giver, not just an intimacy taker.

Solitude prepares me to sit in silence with a loved one. I am not tempted to fill every minute with talk. Nonverbal dialogue gives my conversations more substance. Jesus went into the solitary places, into the quiet places. There He gained strength to bless the people in the marketplaces of His world. Such solitude was His source of inner reinforcement that helped Him to withstand disappointment and rejection by His own disciples. Our Saviour placed His stamp of approval on solitude.

Your first exposures to intentional solitude may be unnerving. The following suggestions will help you to enjoy it from the start.

- Play a musical instrument. I prefer my quiet instruments such as the bowed psaltery, mountain dulcimer, harmonica, and kalimba.
- Whittle a walking stick. My father carved them on the front porch of his mountain home.
- Memorize and sing a hymn.
- Ponder a favorite Bible passage.
- Write a poem.
- Crochet. My mother crocheted rugs for her grandchildren. Her needle flew with little conscious effort.
- Sketch or paint a picture.

- Take a walk and identify as many trees and plants as you can. Use a field guide.
- Sit by a stream and count your blessings.
- Climb a hillside and enjoy the scenery below.
- Curl up on a couch with a good book.
- Make a list of people you want to call or write.
- Walk a beach.
- Find a secluded woods and identify bird calls.
- Go to a U-pick orchard and pick fruit. I like to climb a ladder and select the biggest and ripest fruit. When my basket is full, I sit on the top of the ladder and enjoy the juiciest apple I can find. In blueberry patches I sit under a bush and eat my fill. Then I pay the owner extra.
- Paddle a canoe slowly along the edge of a lake. Practice noiseless paddling so you can observe wildlife.
- Sit on the front porch in your favorite chair. I like to re-live pleasant experiences.

There. Now you can enjoy solitude. Just remember the word *balance*.

CHAPTER SIX

Expectations and Reality

Suzanne was head over heels in love with a handsome U.S. Air Force man. He looked sharp in his uniform. Proud to be in his company, she had highly romantic ideas about marrying a flying ace. She pictured herself snuggled up with her good-looking man, secure in his strong arms, loved passionately by someone who wanted more than anything else to be with her.

Unfortunately Suzanne and Brad never talked about what military life was like. Brad assumed that Suzanne knew about it. He thought that her love and commitment would help her weather the storm of long absences and many moves. Both of them went to the altar without discussing expectations and reality.

After the honeymoon they moved to a tiny apartment near the base. Suzanne had no friends. She had left her support system behind. Just weeks after they moved into the apartment, Brad had a long stint of duty on an aircraft carrier. Alone in a strange place, she spent lots of time in bed thinking about her dreams. The more she thought, the more lonely she became. Her present situation was not what she expected.

When Brad finished his tour of duty, he came home to a woman who was feeling sorry for herself. Although angry, she didn't have the courage to tell Brad about her disappointment and loneliness. A strange silence plagued the marriage that should have been filled with excitement.

Long periods of separation, frequent moves, and difficulties with open communication began to crumble Suzanne's dream. She lived in constant loneliness that threatened to destroy her emotional health.

I met Suzanne in a psychiatric ward, where she was catatonic at times. When she was well enough to visit with me, we had long talks about her dream of eternal romance with her flying ace. We also talked about the nature of military life, especially what it was like for a wife. During the months of her hospitalization she was able to examine her dreams and expectations. Slowly she realized how unrealistic they were. She admitted that she and Brad had never talked about their expectations for marriage, nor did they discuss how they could nurture a new marriage in spite of military uncertainty.

The last leg of her treatment was to have long talks with Brad. They had to engage in serious discussions that should have preceded their wedding. But they adjusted their expectations and decided on ways to maximize the benefits of their time together. Learning how to have real dialogue together, they promised never to hide their true feelings from each other, but to try to be as transparent as they could.

After bringing expectations and reality closer together, Suzanne and Brad began to realize part of their dreams. Some parts had to be put on hold. Other parts they had to discard. A few new dreams evolved. Suzanne brought her loneliness into manageable levels.

Bringing expectations and reality closer together is an important practice in the management of loneliness. Neglecting it has created loneliness in marriage and in many other areas of everyday life.

Someone talked Andrea into taking accounting at a community college. Graduating, she took a job with a large insurance company. A people person, she was excited about making good money and also thought her job would provide interesting social contacts. I met her after she had been on the job for three months.

She now found herself stuck in a back office, where she fought with a computer eight hours a day. Often she ate her lunch at her desk when her computer was giving her problems. When the workday ended, her fellow employees made a dash for the time clocks and the parking lot. Her new job made her feel like she was being confined in a prison. Her loneliness at work carried over into her apartment, where she lived alone.

Andrea was insightful enough to figure out the solution. A people person working in an environment suited for a more retiring person, she decided to look at other professions that would give her the chance to mix with people all day. She planned additional education to put her on the track toward that profession.

Olivia married a professor well known in educational circles. Totally wrapping her life in his, she decided she didn't need friends and interests of her own. The professor was all she needed. Although she really expected him to outlive her so that she could always lean on him, the lingering illness and death of her husband shattered her expectations. In addition to the expected loneliness after a loss, Olivia experienced a loneliness caused by the total absence of supportive relationships.

When she attended one of my support groups, we encouraged her to examine her expectations. She discovered how unrealistic they were. After altering her expectations, she took time to find her own strengths, began to develop those strengths, and set some interesting goals for her life. It was helpful in hurdling the enormous amount of loneliness she was experiencing.

Research psychologists have developed what they call the *discrepancy model* of loneliness. When a discrepancy exists between expectations and reality, loneliness results. While it is not the reason for all loneliness, it certainly accounts for some of it.

One time I had a long conversation with a minister's wife. She had a two-year nursing degree and definite plans to finish a four-year degree. When she married a seminary student, she fully expected to finish her education shortly after her husband took his first assignment.

Unfortunately, the small parish had old-fashioned ideas of what a minister's wife should do. Since her husband's salary was low, he expected her to work to augment the income. By the time she headed up the women's group and planned the annual bazaar, her educational plans went out the window. She felt that the congregation was controlling her whole life. She did not have an ally in her husband, because his expectations of her resembled those of the church. Also, she served as a taxi driver for her two girls, taking them to dance class, games, and 4-H meetings. Loneliness gripped her until she felt powerless to change anything, let alone finish her education.

Finally she and her husband went to see a counselor. Together they resolved the problem. They notified the parish that she would not take more responsibility than she could handle. Limiting their daughters' activities, the couple shared the driving. She trimmed her educational plans, taking just a few classes while the girls were in junior high school. After open communication and altered expectations on the part of all parties, she has been happy about making some progress on her degree. Now that the family is working together, her loneliness is gone.

Some expectations are admirable and worthy of pursuing. They don't need to be changed. But we simply should not expect to achieve them quickly. I compare it to eating a birthday cake. If I ask you to eat your birthday cake in one bite, you will tell me it is impossible. But if I cut the cake into manageable pieces, over time you will be able to eat the whole cake, provided it doesn't become too stale.

Worthwhile expectations can be turned into plans that you can break down into stages. Such a process makes the expectations much more realistic. You are less likely to become lonely. One of the stages may be a waiting period, but as long as the waiting period is time-limited, you will be able to fit it into the whole picture.

Much of the loneliness I experienced in boyhood resulted from great expectations that flew in the face of my parents' low income. Right after World War II I wanted a new bicycle so desperately that I could smell the fresh paint and hear the horn. I had never had a bicycle of my own, but that didn't change my mother's response—"We just can't afford it." I ended up with an old clunker that my brother-in-law sold to me for $5. In addition, I wanted to join the Future Farmers of America and raise a registered Aberdeen Angus steer, but my father was too busy to take me to the meetings, and he couldn't afford a registered animal. As a result I spent many a lonely day dreaming of things that would never come true. My oldest brother talked to me real straight. He told me he could perform the necessary surgery on the next bull calf born to our herd. I could have just as much fun raising a Holstein steer. My brother was right. My steer, Georgie, was so well trained that I could lead him anywhere I liked. One day I brought him into the kitchen and nearly caused my mother to blow a fuse. Looking back, I realize that I saved myself much loneliness by adjusting my expectations.

I've met many of the students attending a college near my home. They had visions of an electrifying social life from the first day of school. Loneliness overtook them when it didn't happen. When they realized that most new college students experience separation anxiety, they lowered their expectations, and the loneliness lessened.

Expectations about a job, marriage, college, a new home, a vacation, or a friendship can escalate far beyond the possibility of real life. It can lead to loneliness when the dream doesn't come true. We would be wise to talk about our expectations with a friend who can help us to get down to earth in our thinking.

As our four boys were growing up, they had some pretty heady expectations. I tried to help them trim them down to size, but at times denial took over their thinking. In spite of what I said, they were headed for disappointment and the resulting loneliness.

I know adults who live with a lot of denial. They plan to build castles when they can afford only a cabin. When the cabin materializes, they find themselves caught in a web of loneliness until they finally see the advantages of living in a cabin.

We can save ourselves from loneliness and disappointment by bringing expectations and reality closer together before we plan to build.

CHAPTER SEVEN

Adolescents and Loneliness

After interviewing hundreds of people who attended bereavement support groups, I have concluded that adolescence is the loneliest time of life. They told me of painful episodes of loneliness as teenagers.

In addition, I have met many lonely teenagers in eating disorders units. They usually lived in strongly enmeshed families in which they were expected to keep the dysfunctional home on an even keel. When the home was in disarray, they received the blame. The result was withdrawal and escape into a negative experience with food.

The spirituality group I conducted became a safe place for them to share their loneliness. They made lists of the losses they experienced. *Family* and *self* usually stood at the top of the list. The young people spoke about these losses with anger and tears. Their description of loneliness brought tears to my own eyes.

Repeatedly it angered me when insurance companies refused to cover more than one or two weeks of treatment. I watched dozens of young women leave the hospital before they knew how to manage their eating disorder or the loneliness. Their support systems were inadequate, and dialogue was nonexistent in their homes.

Such experiences led me to investigate the findings of other researchers. They agreed that adolescence is a real loneliness trap. Now I am on the lookout for lonely adolescents.

A Christian boarding school counselor asked me to meet with a small group of students in crisis. A young man lingered after the group ended.

"How's school going for you?" I asked.

"Gradewise, OK," he offered. "I can't say I really want to be here. Most of my friends go to public school back home."

"What brought you here?"

"My folks divorced and remarried recently. I guess I was in the way, because they are just starting out in new marriages. They both have the money to pay my tuition and all. So here I am."

"Are you fitting in?" I continued.

"Not really. I haven't learned to know anyone. My friends are back home. The kids here seem nice, but I don't go out of my way to meet them. I'd rather be home."

"Are you lonely?"

"Yeah, super lonely."

He was no exception. Letitia Peplau and Daniel Perlman indicate that lonely adolescents commonly report a complex pattern of negative, nonsupportive relationships with their parents. They talk about "parental disinterest, limited nurturance, parental violence and rejection, low levels of encouragement for success, and negative labeling" (*Loneliness*, p. 280).

Adolescent loneliness often has its roots in childhood. Early attachment loss may leave a legacy of loneliness and low self-esteem. Without a secure relationship with parents, children are more likely to have low self-esteem and poor social adjustment that opens the door to loneliness.

THE CRAZY IN-BETWEENS

Adolescents are no longer children, but neither are they adults, meaning that they have lost their previous identity and attachments. Loneliness results until they can reestablish a strong new sense of identity, community, and intimacy.

I remember attending a church picnic when I was 13. A few children younger than I were playing a childish game. Although I joined in for a few minutes, I soon became bored. The adults were organizing a softball game, but I was sure that I could not play well enough to compete. Eventually I ended up roaming around the park by myself.

My neighbor boy was younger than I. He loved to play games of fantasy usually modeled after the latest Wild West movie showing in the town theater. I wasn't interested in fantasy. My newly developing abstract thinking had me laying plans to make money on my father's small farm. When I shared my exciting plans with my father, he always had reasons they wouldn't work. I didn't fit in the world of childish thinking, yet I didn't have the experience to evaluate adult plans.

Pigeons used our barn as the hub of their travel pattern. By now I was 14. I read in a farming magazine that people in the big cities ate pigeon. Immediately I had visions of making big dollars selling pigeons. After scattering a pile of corn on the chicken pen roof, I placed a bushel basket over it that I propped up with a stick. To the stick I attached a long string. When the pigeons visited my trap, I pulled the string and placed them inside the chicken pen. Eventually I had more than 100 pigeons fattening themselves on top-quality chicken feed. The chicken huckster bought all the pigeons, but those lightweight creatures didn't swing the scales enough to yield a big profit. That was one time my father allowed me to try my adult scheme without giving his advice.

In my adolescent years I moved away from my strong child-parent attachments, but I didn't have any other strong attachments to take their place. I distinctly remember longing to know someone intimately, but living on a farm didn't provide many relationships other than family.

A few times I attempted to develop friendships with boys on nearby farms, but my father held the strings tightly. He was afraid that I would get into bad company. He'd always say, "A boy is a boy. Two boys is half a boy. Three boys is no boy at all. I think you'd better stay home and do your work."

Caught in the crazy in-betweens, I was not a part of the child's world, yet I was not allowed into the world of adulthood. Social and emotional isolation resulted, and I was lonely.

Burgeoning Intimacy Needs

Adolescents have a new interpersonal need for intimacy that can lead to intense loneliness. Voluntary departure from close child-parent ties leaves a vacuum that may not get filled soon enough to avoid loneliness. Social skills are still often underdeveloped, making the formation of new intimacies and a new community difficult. Intense crushes on the opposite sex are abundant. Young people often view failure to have a boyfriend or girlfriend as a personal flaw. Adolescents move quickly from one relationship to another, because they are awkward and bungling in them. They are learning a yet-unmastered art.

Often adolescents have unrealistic expectations of relationships. They truly expect the bells and whistles to go off in every one. They also expect to have a superabundance of friendships as well. Reality easily shatters their expectations.

A classmate who lived in the dormitory with me is a classic example. He was 17 and madly in love with a minister's daughter. In his mind he had vivid pictures of dating this girl, who would sweep him off his feet and meet every need he ever felt. When the day of the first date arrived, he was on cloud nine, but after the date he returned to the dormitory in the pit of despondency. Taught to be very proper with boys, the girl had not perfected her social skills, was quite shy, and had shattered all of his mental pictures. Now he sat on his dormitory cot sulking. When his roommate asked why he was so glum, he picked up a shoe and threw it through a window.

My friend may be an extreme example, but adolescents do have high expectations of their relationships. Some researchers think that's the reason older people are not as lonely as adolescents. Most have learned to have more realistic expectations.

I have talked with young adults now unhappy with their marriages because they carried highly impractical and unrealistic expectations of relationships from adolescence into later life. They were convinced that every day should be a day of bells and whistles.

MAKING MUD PIES

When I was a child, my sisters and I made mud pies. In our minds we were serving a noble purpose. We delivered our products to imaginary homes, where children ate the sweet delights and asked for more. Running a bakery was a rewarding experience. That's because we were children.

Adolescents take no delight in menial and nonessential roles. Their days of mud pies are over, but they have a difficult time convincing adults that they have the potential for tasks that make a difference. Tim Brennan observes that adolescents experience blocked participation in valued activities and roles, which leads to social isolation and loneliness (*Loneliness*, p. 277).

I know adolescents who would like to have a part-time job doing something rewarding, but all they can find is low-paying work at fast-food restaurants. They do repetitive jobs such as flipping burgers and dipping french fries. Their bosses push them to work faster and seldom give their young employees affirmation or appreciation. If they don't like the pressure, the bosses can quickly replace them. My young friends tell me they hate such mindless tasks, but nobody seems willing to harness their assets for meaningful work.

A friend and I had experience painting houses and barns. We decided to start a painting business to help pay for our tuition, but ran into a snag. Because we were young, people in our church didn't think we should receive the going rates for painting a room. The custodian of the church hired us to paint the huge choir room with a 12-foot ceiling. I was standing on a tall stepladder rolling the ceiling when the pastor and the custodian entered.

"What are these boys receiving for this job?" the pastor inquired.

"Three dollars per hour," the custodian responded.

"Three dollars?" the startled pastor asked.

The custodian thought a moment and replied, "If you'd like, sir, I'd be glad to give the job to a local firm for $6 per hour."

The pastor left the room muttering to himself about paying students outrageous wages. The custodian stayed behind to compliment us on the good job we were doing. I still remember how tall and important Mr. Mayes made us feel that day. Also I discovered that day why young people did not like that pastor.

I belong to a denomination that believes in giving young people a piece of the pie, yet I know of local congregations who will not spend money on a decent youth room. They'll buy a new organ and install an expensive stained-glass window, but relegate the youth to a dingy back room. Adolescents are not blind. They can feel rejection and know when they are being blocked from participating in valued activities and roles. And they feel the isolation. Loneliness is no stranger to adolescents in this kind of church.

Exciting opportunities are becoming available to adolescents in my church and other faith communities. Serious young adults can take short-term mission trips to Puerto Rico, Belize, Mexico, Dominican Republic, Haiti, and low-income parts of the United States of America. They lay cement blocks and bricks, pour cement, frame buildings, and install roofing. Others accompany physicians and dentists to remote villages, where they actually dress wounds, pull teeth, fit people with glasses, and take vital signs. Besides that, they lead worship services and conduct Vacation Bible Schools.

Two of my sons have gone on such mission trips. I have helped to finance mission trips for a number of the youth in my congregations. Frequently I have heard them say that the trips made them feel useful. They knew they were not doing busywork, but service that made a difference in the lives of others. Here is the way to give adolescents meaning and purpose that will keep loneliness from invading their lives.

Once I visited a school for troubled American adolescents located in an island country. I had plenty of time to interview the students. They told me they had no sense of purpose in the United States, no meaningful roles in which they performed selfless service. Boredom and loneliness were constant.

But in their new island home that changed. They accompanied a public health doctor to little mountain villages. The doctor put them to work in his clinics. Young people served as orderlies and aides in the hospital near the school. Culture shock had an indelible effect on them as they worked in the maternity ward with two new mothers sleeping on one army cot. They shooed the chickens out of the hospital lobby and scrubbed the cement floors by dumping buckets of river water on them and swishing the water around with a broom.

Some of the youth graduated from that school and later returned to serve on the staff. They discovered their potential and found a role that prevented further boredom and loneliness.

Adolescents constantly experience the emergence of new potentialities for which they seek important and appropriate outlets. If they do not find such outlets, they may feel bored, aimless, restless—a condition sometimes called spiritual loneliness.

Churches would be wise to reduce institutionalization and increase local ministry to youth. If they can prevent spiritual loneliness, the adolescents will be loyal to the church and become a positive force for good in their communities.

The Competitive Rat Race

Adolescents encounter competition very early. Grading, athletic activities, social functions that expect dating, tryouts for musical organizations, and other activities that emphasize competitive individualism set some adolescents up for rejection, failure, isolation, and loneliness.

When I lived in Massachusetts, ice hockey was a real craze. Parents insisted on their children joining peewee teams. An ice rink near my home was in use around the clock. Peewee teams began practicing at 5:00 a.m., because ice time was scarce. Teachers told me about grade school students falling asleep in class. The competition between the teams was fierce. Defeat was a shame.

Some advocates of a competitive lifestyle say that it prepares a person to make a living in the real world, but competition at an early age can also be damaging. Adolescents don't all have the same skills. When pressured to compete, they can face humiliation that pushes them to withdraw.

I attended a high school where softball was the only activity available at noontime. The teachers insisted that all the students play. That placed me in a real predicament. A farmboy who seldom played ball, I had poor coordination. When I didn't strike out, I popped the ball up to the infielders and seldom stepped on first base. The team captains didn't want me on their team. Sometimes they would change the batting order to keep me from batting during the entire noon hour. I knew what they were doing and why, and it damaged my self-concept.

When I was a young minister attending annual retreats, the big event was a ball game. My peers urged me to play, but I gave all sorts of excuses. Usually I made my way to the horseshoe pits, where I played with the senior citizens in ministry. Eventually I learned to avoid the feelings of loneliness by taking a walk when it was time to start the ball game.

Personal experience has proved to me that competition can encourage loneliness in adolescence. And it can do the same for adults.

I take my hat off to a church youth club director who believes that every local club should leave a camporee with a trophy. Cooperation, not competition, is the principle behind the trophy. Every club member can look at the trophy and feel an important part of the achievement. This director is to be commended for ditching the competitive rat race.

RELATIONSHIP BUILDING

Studies done among adolescents who are consistently lonely show that they have problems in all areas of interpersonal relationships. Besides having difficulty relating to peers, parents, and teachers, they seldom experience personal success in forming lasting friendships. Henri Nouwen feels that it may be because of a lack of transgenerational experience. We tend to segregate people by age in many areas of life, robbing us of lessons we could learn from persons with more experience.

I learned a valuable lesson in making friends from a chaplain much older than I. He had taken no clinical training, as I had, but he had learned a secret I needed.

"Kimber," I said, "how is it that every patient in this hospital loves you? They ask about you when I enter their rooms."

"I'll tell you a secret I learned a long time ago. It works with both agreeable people and disagreeable people. I ask them about their work, their place of origin, and their children. All people love to talk about these parts of their life. I just sit back and listen. Then I try to remember what they tell me so I can mention it during a subsequent visit."

I think adolescents could benefit from training in building relationships. If they learned such things as those Kimber shared with me, they might be spared much heartache and loneliness. Why not offer classes in social skills in grade school and continue them into high school?

SELF-ESTEEM

While we are teaching social skills, we need to help adolescents build healthy self-esteem. Most of the research I examined on loneliness indicated that lonely people suffer from low self-esteem, though debate rages about whether low self-esteem causes loneliness or whether loneliness leads to low self-esteem.

I know this has been the topic of many books, but we still have not mastered the art of building it into the lives of our children and adolescents. What will it take to accomplish it?

Perhaps we should teach parenting skills as part of premarital counseling. After all, childbearing is a likely possibility after marriage. Wouldn't it be responsible to learn how to equip a child for life?

Also, why not examine our theology of sin and redemption? What about those hymns that call people worms and wretches? Would God plan to save His children if they had no inherent value?

Maybe we need to broaden our view of spiritual gifts and recognize the simpler, less noticeable gifts so ably exercised by children and adolescents. Openness, transparency, and sensitivity are gifts I treasure in the youth of my churches. The gift of playfulness—how about recognizing that one?

Five earliteens pestered me to play hide-and-seek in the dark. Sabbath vespers had just ended. They needed to let off steam that had built up during the day of rest. One of them noticed my reticence and pleaded, "Please, Pastor Larry, it's part of your job. Pastors are supposed to play with kids." That sounded like a pretty sensible part of a minister's job description. I played until I was totally winded. You know what? I think my earliteens felt worthwhile because I recognized their gift of playfulness.

Here's a great idea. Why not quit calling adolescents the church of tomorrow? If we made them part of the church today, they might feel good about their value.

I have a self-esteem builder that I use every day. Watching for young people, I sit next to them and engage them in conversation. I tell them that I like them and thank them for sharing their ideas with me. I listen to them more than I speak.

Once I went to a convention in British Columbia. Sitting by himself in the lodge was a young man who had had one hand amputated. A local boy, he often came to warm himself by the fireplace. I noticed that people avoided him. Maybe they didn't know what to say to a person with an amputation. Sitting on the couch with him, I asked him what type of work he did. He told me he was a driver for a lumbering company. Without my inquiring he told me he had lost his hand in a sawmill accident. He said the mill was paying for his retraining. In the meantime he was driving to make a little money for his parents. They were sickly and needed his help.

When the supper bell rang, I invited him to eat with me. Before we parted that day, I told him how grateful I was to him for making me feel welcome. In addition, I complimented him for his commitment to his family and for his determination to learn a new trade. I could see self-esteem growing within his chest as I spoke.

During the next two days that young man sought me out and chatted with me. We ate together. Although I was old enough to be his father, he believed he had something to offer me.

I have a hunch that we could erase much of the adolescent loneliness if we all made it our mission to allow youth to teach us. They have as much to give us as we have to offer them, but we have to let them know that we are willing to learn.

They Are Survivors

I don't want to give the impression that most adolescents suffer from chronic or despairing loneliness. The largest percentage of teens learn social skills and become adept at making the transition from childhood to adulthood without a strong sense of isolation. In spite of negative societal factors they find a useful and rewarding role in the community. They are survivors.

But I do want to get across that the lonely adolescents are too valuable to ignore. If we do not address their predicament, they could be headed for physical and emotional illness or even premature death.

CHAPTER EIGHT

Elder Loneliness

Nellie happily showed me her diploma from a correspondence school. She had majored in journalism. Proudly she displayed a book of poetry she had published and a manuscript soon to be submitted to a major publisher. Her favorite poem was about a young girl who went skinny-dipping in the village pond. The picture with the poem showed a girl's dress hanging on a bush and a girl swimming in the pond. I asked her who the girl was. It was she. Another poem told about riding a motorcycle. Again, she was the rider of the Indian motorcycle.

President of the residents' association at the nursing home where she lived, Nellie took the grievances of the residents to the owners of the home. Also, she taught in-service training for the staff on how residents perceive having to live in a nursing home. She was 90.

Across the hall from Nellie resided Arlene. After a short greeting she looked up at the ceiling and said, "Do you think I'm going to die soon?"

"Why do you ask?" I queried.

"I just want to hurry up and die and get it over with. I'm sick and tired of being alone and cold," she replied.

Arlene had no family. She had no interests and seldom

talked with anyone. Desperately lonely, she was also 90.

Nellie was not lonely, while Arlene was. I asked myself if most elders were like Nellie or like Arlene. So I made it a point to spend lots of time with elders in the hospital, the nursing and retirement homes, and in the community. My findings surprised me.

"Chaplain, I wish you'd stop in to visit Mr. Bradshaw in 211. We try to visit with him, but he goes to sleep on us in a matter of moments." The nurse was truly concerned.

I lingered near Room 211 that day just to hear the employees talking with him. Every person who entered his room spoke to him like a mother would speak to a tiny baby. True to form, he feigned sleep.

When I visited the man, I decided to treat him as I would any intelligent person. "Mr. Bradshaw, I have a strong inclination to believe that you are a very competent businessman. What was your trade?"

"I was a foreman in a large lumber company in Oregon with 70 men working under me," he explained. "I had a very responsible position. Many things hung on my performance, and I did a good job for the company. I retired from there after 35 years with the company." He had a pleased look on his face as he told me.

"You need to teach me some lessons, Mr. Bradshaw," I said. "How do you manage 70 men and keep their cooperation and respect?"

"I've always maintained that a man in management must not be afraid of hard work. I put my muscle to the job right along with the men under me. I think that's the answer to good management."

From there the conversation turned to the product line of his company and trends in the lumber industry. Mr. Bradshaw spoke with authority and confidence. After a half hour he showed signs of tiring. Quietly excusing himself, he went to sleep.

After visiting with hundreds of elders, I am convinced that, like Mr. Bradshaw, they disengage from society because society disengages from them. People often treat them like simple-minded children. In an effort to preserve their own dignity, they disengage, rather than let themselves be demeaned. Loneliness results from such disengagement, but the disengagement can be broken.

I visited a disengaged elder for 30 minutes every day for weeks. She repeated a nonsense phrase and played annoyingly with the hem of her housecoat. All my questions seemed to fall on deaf ears, but I persisted in asking intelligent questions. I told her stories about my life and why I liked to visit her. Sometimes I told her funny stories and jokes.

After a few weeks of steady visitation, she placed her hands on my cheeks and said, "You are a silly man." I knew she had reengaged. It excited me to watch her blossom.

The Arlenes among elders are in the minority. Many of them are lonely because they do not receive social stimulation. People do not treat them as valuable, intelligent human beings.

Researchers observe that loneliness diminishes with age. Life experience teaches us to adjust to losses and deficits. Our expectations of relationships are more realistic than they were when we were young. Even though our community diminishes, our changing expectations reduce the amount of loneliness.

Frequently I ask audiences what age group is the loneliest in America. They often guess old age. That may be their response because they visit nursing homes and see the elderly people shuffling up and down the halls or sitting in their chairs. Many of the residents do not have contentment written on their faces.

An old woman sat by the door of her nursing home every day. As people entered it, she would ask, "Can anyone teach me to be happy?" The men who were with me one day left that home with the impression that all elderly people are unhappy, but that isn't true. I spent years visiting all the residents in one nursing home. I found that most of them were quite happy and content with their situation.

While the percentage of elderly people in nursing homes is still in the single digits, this statistic should not make us comfortable. As long as one elder is lonely, we should make efforts to respond to that loneliness. The small percentage of American elders in nursing homes can easily suffer because of the out-of-sight-out-of-mind mind-set. Churches and other volunteer agencies should keep them in mind.

I do some training for a group of healthy seniors. Their goal is to find every lonely person in Lansing, Michigan, and minister to their needs. Because elders experience many losses, the volunteers are not always able to distance themselves therapeutically. My role is to help the volunteers grieve for their own personal losses so that they can comfort the elderly clients without personalizing their pain.

When I was the volunteer chaplain for a nursing home, I discovered a way to use transgenerational contact to bring purpose and meaning back into the lives of elderly people. We used reminiscing therapy. I gathered a group of young people ranging anywhere from five to 20 in number. They joined me at the nursing home. On a round table in the center of the room I placed an old-fashioned tablecloth and a kerosene lamp. Around the table I placed many items that the elders probably used or saw when they were children. The elders gathered in a small circle around the table, and the youth formed an outer circle around them. One by one I held up the objects and had the elders tell what they remembered about each item.

Next I did the same with music, asking the elders to teach the young people the songs of their childhood. Then I asked the young people to teach the elders one of their catchy choruses.

Since the kerosene lamp was the center of attraction, I asked the elders to relate stories of their life involving the kerosene lamp. They told about doing their homework by lamp, eating evening meals by the glow of a lamp, and playing board games. Frequently they mentioned snuggling with boyfriends or girlfriends away from the brightest rays of the lamp. I always concluded our sessions by inviting one elder to blow out the kerosene lamp. Sometimes I had to relight the lamp several times until all who wished had a chance to extinguish the flame.

Reminiscing therapy could easily become a memorable part of a church party for the elderly members, but remembering the past is not the only thing elders wish to do. Some have a desire to operate a computer. Why not have a computer class for these church members? I frequently have older people tell me that computers mystify them. Imagine how excited they would be to enter the new age of computers. Older people will be less lonely if they can be part of the present.

Once I was attending a hospital board meeting when I met a brilliant former church leader. He was a board member. The chairman of the board asked him if current church leaders called on him for advice. He said, "No, in this church a retired church leader is forgotten. I see some of the mistakes that the current leaders make, but nobody asks me for my opinion."

I think we could reduce loneliness among the elderly if we used them on boards and committees. What about a church advisory board comprised of retired people? Remaining useful in the church could prevent loneliness.

Elderly people in my churches have been my best advisers. I am indebted to them for giving me encouragement, correction, and some terrific ideas. Also, I've been surprised by how many of them happily encouraged the participation of the youth of the church.

In addition, elderly people know how to engage in life at a slowed but satisfying pace. The annual fair at Centreville, Michigan, featured a draft horse competition in 1996. I sat in the grandstands and watched the whole event. The four-mule hitch had two entries, a son and his 93-year-old father. The judge carefully watched both teams and the teamsters as they trotted and walked on command. After careful deliberation, the judge proclaimed the father and his team the prize winners. The father trotted his team around the corral one last time. Finally pulling his team to a halt next to the judge, he asked, "Is there anything else you want me to do?"

The judge replied, "Yes. Be sure you enter your team next year at the Centreville Fair." The audience clapped and whistled in agreement.

That judge learned from that old gentleman, who had been at the fair for 29 years in a row. No doubt that old mule driver had much more to teach the judge about judging.

When I left home to attend school, I needed a mother. I met an 81-year-old woman in a retirement home near the college. She took a liking to me and I to her. Each time I acquired a new girlfriend, I took her to see Mrs. Massey. The next day I'd drop in to hear her evaluation. If I was homesick, her cheerfulness always lifted me. A concert pianist, she could appreciate my interest in choral work and band performance. She loved to tell me about nearly missing a concert when a river overflowed its banks, but managing to arrive at the concert hall by rowboat. Mrs. Massey approved when I became engaged. I respected her judgment.

At the time I did not realize how important my trust was to Mrs. Massey. Now I realize it made her feel that she was still productive. She was my mother-away-from-home and my teacher. As Henri Nouwen put it, "only when we are able to receive the elderly as our teachers will it be possible to offer the help they are looking for" (*Aging*, p. 153).

CHAPTER NINE

Loneliness in Marriage and Divorce

I f I were giving advice to a young person about marriage, I
would tell him or her to find someone who is as much like
himself or herself as possible. It's often said that opposites
attract, but it's not a good idea for opposites to marry. A good
chance exists that marrying someone with many opposite interests and values could usher you into married loneliness.

My denomination has many women whose husbands do
not share their faith. They attend church alone and raise children in the church alone. Faith is the most personal part of life.
If you can't share it with your spouse, you may experience
spiritual loneliness.

Quite often the wife faces subtle criticisms of her faith.
Sometimes she encounters open anger. It can often go on year
after year until other areas of her marriage become dissatisfying.

A wife told me that her husband was surly from the beginning of her Sabbath until the end of it. Another described
how her husband planned projects around the house that
would make it impossible to spend a quiet Sabbath. One
woman told me that her husband left the house on Friday afternoon and didn't return until late Saturday night.

Opposite values separate spouses and make loneliness a
reality. One goes to bars, and the other cannot bring himself or

herself to enter one. A husband spends money on car racing and sits in the bleachers watching the races twice a week, and the wife disapproves of wasting money on such senseless entertainment. Opposite values take spouses down separate roads. Loneliness eats away until resentment and depression overwhelm the life.

Values determine the activities in which we are interested. If two people have opposite values, they will have little or nothing to experience together. It destroys the friendship level of the marriage and makes it difficult to understand the emotions of the person with whom you live.

A man became deeply involved in driving four-wheel off-road vehicles. He joined a club that had many weekend excursions with the guys. Driving on rough terrain meant expensive repairs that dipped into the food budget and the clothing allowance. His wife, stuck at home with the children, became angry, depressed, and lonely.

The preceding examples are just a few of the dozens of people I've met. They seem to be at an impasse in their marriage. Loneliness crippled one or both of the spouses, and nothing seems to be done about it. The longer it goes on, the more it stamps sick patterns on the marriage. Someone in the marriage must break the gridlock. That could be done by confronting in love. Here's how you might go about it.

Make a date with your spouse when you will have privacy and plenty of time. Let him or her know that you are doing this because you have something crucial to share. Begin the session by asking the spouse to listen without interrupting. Assure him or her that when you are finished you will give your spouse the floor without interruption. Tell him or her that you are doing this because you love him or her and because you cherish your relationship. Let him or her know that what you say is based on what you feel, that the possibility exists that some of your feelings may not be justified, and that all your comments are coming from a heart that really cares and loves.

Without attacking him or her, tell how you feel about the circumstances. Specify what you think would be a possible solution. Clearly indicate that you must see the problem re-solved if you are to be a happy spouse. Let him or her know that you expect to come to some solution that both of you will take seriously. Strongly encourage joint marriage counseling as a way of speedily moving toward a solution. Don't finish until you tell the other one the part you have also played in bringing the marriage to a very lonely and unhappy state. You should also tell him or her what you are willing to do to change it. Let your spouse know that you are willing to pray with him or her about a solution.

The last part of this confrontation is to allow the other person to take all the time he or she needs to speak without interruption. Don't begin any kind of planning until after the spouse states that he or she is finished. You may want to have a time for both of you to respond before the planning begins.

Many of the men and women I have listened to tell me that this loving confrontation method has worked for them. If you want to break the marriage loneliness, it takes confrontation, not battle. Angry discussions deepen the alienation and the loneliness. But loving confrontation lets your spouse know what your needs are and how they can be met. Just be sure that you don't make unfair demands. Don't hang on to unrealistic expectations.

I have discovered that if two people concentrate on restoring and strengthening their friendship, their values will come closer together. They will have common interests that keep them friends. In that process of developing friendship, loneliness lessens.

WHAT ABOUT DIVORCE?

After I presented a seminar on loneliness, a young mother of two asked to chat. She described the total isolation she had felt when she lived with a man who was emotionally ill. The situation worsened until she was afraid of being murdered in her sleep. He eventually violated his marriage vows and agreed to a divorce.

Unfortunately, divorce did not lessen her loneliness. Her

couple-friends no longer invited her to social events, and her local church congregation didn't have single parents her age. Because she worked hard to support the children, it meant she was tired, too tired to be interested in socializing. Responsibility to her children demanded that she stay busy, which meant that she never grieved for the marriage she had hoped to have but never did. The woman came to the place where she was depressed and could not sleep. When I spoke to her, she was desperate for answers. She said her loneliness made her feel that she was floating through space with no destination.

I consistently recommend professional counseling to the divorced lonely. Loss through divorce is too traumatic to handle alone. You need to get on with life, but you need to have someone guide you gently at a time when you are helpless and lonely.

I'm going to make a suggestion that involves the determined effort of the divorced person. Also I'm going to challenge the church to take the loneliness of divorce to heart.

The church has poured much energy, planning, technology, and promotion into global evangelism, women's ministry, men's ministry, children's ministry, and to a lesser extent youth ministry. Divorce recovery programs and grief recovery programs are a different story. Although used occasionally, often they have been employed as a means of interesting nonchurched people in joining the church.

Many hours of listening to people with marriage loneliness and divorce loneliness has taught me that they have not been able to get a grip on life again. They don't have the energy to care for their families and certainly don't have what it takes to involve themselves in church work or discipling. These people have been wounded, but the church leaves them in the trenches to die spiritually, emotionally, socially, and physically.

I would challenge those suffering from such loneliness to plead with church leaders for help. And I would challenge church leaders to engage well-trained professionals in a thorough, multifaceted, and continual program aimed at helping such members regain their equilibrium.

A large Methodist church in Fort Worth, Texas, has a comprehensive program to meet the needs of the lonely people. It is more than a social club. Study groups, group counseling, individual counseling, classes in personal growth, hobby learning, parenting classes, and many other related activities fill its monthly calendar.

Why can't other churches do the same? It is a problem that is too complex just to drop in the individual's lap. We must face this problem together in the Christian community. The apostle Paul said that the body is made up of many parts. If one part hurts, it affects the whole body. The whole body must respond to the hurt part. Failure to do so will spell disaster for the sufferers.

Paul also told us to comfort others with the comfort with which God comforts us. It seems to me that Paul gave us the challenge years ago.

CHAPTER TEN

Are There Solutions?

People have approached the loneliness problem in many ways. Research circles have discussed many theories about what causes it. Most of the energy has directed itself toward finding the causes, with much less effort going to treatment and prevention.

I am not condemning the researchers. After all, studies of loneliness began only recently. And the work already done has opened our understanding of the problem. Authorities in this field are fully aware that we need to do more research, including approaches to treatment and prevention. We should be grateful for the strides such dedicated scholars have made.

Here are some of the prominent theories. Since loneliness is such a multifaceted experience, and since all of us are so unique, most or all of these theories could be correct.

- Loneliness results from negative early influences that affect our inner self, our mental health.
- Poor psychosocial development during childhood and adolescence leads to loneliness.
- If people can overcome the fear of loneliness, it can then be a positive force for personal growth.
- Loneliness comes from societal expectations that adversely affect the development of our meaningful relation-

ships. When we do not meet the expectations of others, we feel isolated and become self-blaming.

● A combination of personality factors and situational factors, both internal forces and external forces, produce loneliness.

● The way we perceive ourselves, our situations, and our environment shapes loneliness. What one person sees as loneliness may not constitute loneliness for another.

● Loneliness surfaces when we don't have enough intimate relationships that provide opportunity to disclose our private lives.

● Loneliness is like a barometer that notifies us that our level of human contact has become inadequate.

● We can become lonely by comparing our social relationships with the relationships of others, something particularly true of adolescents and young adults.

● Loneliness can undergo modifications until it becomes chronic and characterized by hopeless apathy.

● A cluster of feelings, behaviors, and thoughts, not one single characteristic, identifies loneliness.

In view of the many concepts of loneliness, it seems wise to look at a number of solutions in our hope that loneliness will lose its death grip on us.

When I conducted smoking-cessation clinics, the physician and I suggested dozens of tips for quitting. We knew that not all of them would aid everyone. After all, every person who smokes does so for a different reason. Our goal was to give ample help so that specific individuals could find what they needed to break their addiction.

I share the following suggestions with you in the hope that some of them will free you from the paralysis of loneliness.

KEEP A LONELINESS JOURNAL

A number of therapists believe that discovering the reason for your loneliness allows you to make sense out of the distressing experience. They see this as the first step in alleviating loneliness. Keeping a loneliness journal is an excellent way to do this. Include the following information in your journal:

- What your loneliness feels like.
- What event seemed to trigger it?
- If this loneliness has been around for some time, what sustains it?
- State the cause of your loneliness in a sentence.
- Is the cause internal or external or both?
- How changeable is the cause of your loneliness?
- Write down several anticipated solutions. Include the time when you will put them into action.
- Does the cause of your loneliness stem from your behavior or your personality? Write a prayer to God for His power to change, then consult a friend or counselor who can help you grow.

STUDY LONELINESS

My work in psychiatric units and bereavement support groups forced me to study the topic. The more I learned about loneliness, the more successful I was in meeting personal loneliness. Knowledge removed fear. When fear was gone, I could face loneliness more constructively.

ADMIT YOUR LONELINESS

Denial is self-defeating. You don't have to be ashamed of being lonely. If you admit it, you'll be motivated to begin your loneliness journal. You'll be on the first leg of your journey to better health.

To deny loneliness guarantees that you will postpone any remedial action. It could turn transient loneliness into a long-lasting problem.

Loneliness is not a sign of weakness. Every human has experienced it in one form or another. We are all in the proverbial boat together, but so often we don't want to admit it.

During bereavement programs I have often asked participants to fill out loneliness surveys. One of the items on the survey says "I am seldom lonely." Many will check that item, but in subsequent personal conversations they inadvertently reveal that they are indeed lonely. I try to make them feel normal by letting them know that I am sometimes lonely myself. Once they admit to being lonely, we have something with which to work. We can set about finding solutions.

ENROLL IN ASSERTIVENESS TRAINING

No, assertiveness is not a four-letter word. It is not rudeness training or learning how to get everything you want. A good trainer will help you to:

- identify your assets—your strengths
- show genuine interest in others
- introduce yourself or others
- give and receive compliments gracefully
- share a different view without judging the opinions of others
- use all the levels of communication, such as chitchat, information gathering, and sharing your deeper self
- know when and how much to disclose yourself
- know how to protect your own dignity and respect that of others

Some loneliness can stem, in part, from a lack of social skills. Assertiveness training develops such skills. It will improve your ability to develop links with others, help you overcome shyness, and improve your self-image.

A friend felt trapped in her job, but she was too shy to tell her boss. After a few short lessons in assertiveness, she approached him: "Dr. Smith, I think I know how I can be a greater asset to your business. You see, I'm really a people person, but the job I'm doing now keeps me in the back room working on assembly and repair of glasses. Lately I have become bored. I'm afraid the quality of my work doesn't measure up to the high standards you have set for your business. If the opportunity comes for working with customers, I think I could make them feel special and pampered. I'll respect your judgment in this matter, but I do hope you'll give it some consideration."

The doctor came to her a few days later and offered to send her to be trained in customer relations. She ended up with a job that challenged her. The boredom left. She credited her change to her few lessons in assertiveness.

Before you enroll in assertiveness training, ask questions about the trainers and their particular concept of assertiveness. Some have given this type of training a bad name, but don't write off this suggestion just because of it. Responsible assertive behavior does harmonize with the principles of the Christian life. Learning such behavior can lift some of the loneliness we face in our competitive high-tech age.

WORK ON SELF-ESTEEM

The most consistent finding in loneliness research is that lonely people suffer from low self-esteem. Improving yourself or your view of yourself would appear to be the solution, but it has its dangers. Some people inaccurately blame their own behaviors and personality. In their attempt to pick themselves up, they put themselves down. They feel powerless to change, and give up trying.

Self-esteem should not rest on how others see us or even on how we regard ourselves. We can be like a yo-yo when it comes to self-evaluation. True esteem has its basis in how God views us. The same yesterday, today, and forever, His view of us never changes. Studying the plan of redemption teaches us how priceless we are. Luke 15 is my favorite Bible passage. When I read it, I can see myself through the eyes of the shepherd, the woman, and the father. The passage gives me a more accurate idea of how much I am worth. I know I can't trust my own judgment of my value, but I can trust the judgment of the One who gave me life.

Satan wants us to question God's judgment. I think he realizes that once low self-esteem gains a foothold, it feeds on itself, causing perceptions that keep it alive and well.

Researchers have found that people with low self-esteem are more passive and overly sensitive to criticism that confirms their own feelings of inadequacy. Such individuals are less popular and more socially anxious, finding it hard to accept compliments. When they look at themselves in a mirror, they see themselves as inept. Reluctant to take risks in a social setting, they are less likely to start new relationships and strengthen existing ones. They are inaccurate judges of their own social skills.

Since low self-esteem perpetuates itself, we are wise to change our criteria for personal worth. Accept God's evaluation of human worth and see if it doesn't reduce loneliness.

I encourage participants in my bereavement support groups to engage in an exercise that recognizes and acknowledges personal worth. You will probably find it helpful. With the aid of a trusted family member or friend, prepare a list of your personal assets. Make another list of the many ways in which those assets have been used to help others. A third list could enumerate ways in which you could employ your assets in the future. Whenever you begin to think disparagingly about yourself, pull out your list and put the negative messages to rest.

Lonely people may play negative self-messages again and again in their minds. They usually verbalize them to others, further ingraining them in their thinking. I have an exercise I do with lonely people.

When a lonely person says "Every relationship I ever had turned sour; I'll never be able to make a lasting friendship," I insist on the individual's substantiating that statement. If he or she can't prove it, I insist on his or her scrapping the idea.

I have found that many lonely people distort their own deficits. But when they have to demonstrate their image of themselves, they discover how distorted their claims really are.

One day a student nurse burst into my office. "I am a stupid failure. I knew I should never have taken the nursing course. I'm nothing but a failure. I'll never make it. I'm through. I know I am. I can't go on."

After I calmed her down, I said, "Stupid failure, eh? Prove it. Prove it to me right now."

"Well, I feel stupid. What other reasons could there have been for making such a dumb medication error?" She sat in the chair, wringing her hands and looking at the floor.

"I'll tell you what I want you to do," I said finally.

"Tomorrow bring all your grade cards from elementary school, high school, and the college courses you've had so far. You and I are going to do a little math."

She agreed. The next day we tapped the numbers into a calculator and found her to be a B student. That's when I said, "That relieves my mind. Now I know that you aren't stupid. I don't want you ever to say that about yourself again."

That conversation took place almost 20 years ago. Just a week before I wrote this chapter, I met her in a hospital. She was ministering to the medical needs of one of my parishioners. Her nursing skills appeared to be well honed. As the patient spoke well of her, my mind reviewed the conversation we had had years ago.

The connection between low self-esteem and loneliness is so strong that I encourage lonely people to seek assistance in changing their evaluation of themselves. A pastor, a caring friend, or a counselor can aid them. Seek help. It can make a difference in the amount of loneliness you experience.

A DAY OF REST

James P. Flanders pointed out a factor in loneliness that took me by surprise. "The decline of a day of rest free of most commerce reduces emotional intimacy and increases loneliness" (*Loneliness*, p. 166).

Our all-wise God provided us with such a day—the Sabbath. It is more than a memorial of Creation. The day of rest provides time to broaden our relationship with God. Twenty-four hours without work and commerce allows time to reflect on our value as God's children. Unhurried socializing with family and friends helps to build intimacy. Time to freely study our natural surroundings shows us that we are part of God's larger scheme.

The prophet Isaiah talks about Sabbath rest (see especially Isaiah 58) as a source of joy and nurture. If Sabbath rest reduces loneliness, it is easy to appreciate the prophet's assessment of Sabbath blessings.

A day of rest enhances human contact and contact with

God. It lifts family relationships and friendships above commercial institutions. Sabbath allows you to place interpersonal relationships above the rush to acquire money and things.

I would suggest that a broader understanding of Sabbath is necessary to allay loneliness. Abstaining from work on Sabbath is not sufficient. Joyful fellowship with family and friends, acts of mercy to others, and spontaneous praise to the Creator will prevent damaging loneliness.

TURN OFF THE TUBE

Flanders also states that the process of household televiewing has become the single most time-consuming activity other than sleep. One researcher estimated that an American who lives to be 75 will have spent 57 years watching TV. If that is true, TV watching would appear to be an addiction.

Watching TV reduces human eye contact, the sharing of feelings, physical and sexual contact, talking and listening to others, family outings, and family rituals (family worship, bedtime stories, mealtimes together, walks together, sharing a book, going to bed at the same time).

Turn off the tube. You'll have more time to develop and enhance interpersonal relationships.

DECIDE YOU WON'T BE DRIVEN

Many lonely people find themselves driven to find someone they think will take away their loneliness. They go from place to place with that one goal in mind. Others sense their desperation for friendship. Their anxiety sometimes causes behavior that repels others instead of bringing them closer. Then the lonely people struggle with the strong temptation to give up.

During those times you don't feel so intensely lonely, make a strong decision that you will not allow yourself desperately to seek friends to save you from loneliness. Decide that you will be friendly as a general rule. And vow that you will show genuine interest in others whenever and wherever you meet them. Relax and tell yourself that lasting friendships take time to grow.

Instead of being driven by anxiety, spend your energy learning valuable social skills that will make friendship formation easier. You can do this by reading good books on the topic. Or you might find a good course at a local college. Some high schools teach a course in relationship building.

In my work with bereaved people I meet many men who anxiously search for another mate shortly after their spouses die. They remarry months, not years, after the death, upsetting their children, who accuse them of remarrying before their mother's body was cold. The men report to me that they were too lonely and had to find another companion.

Lonely people, no matter what the cause, are prone to seek an intimate, long-term relationship early in their lonely state. But that is not advisable. Such individuals often wind up living with a person they cannot get along with.

It is much better to make your first priority engaging in pleasurable solitary activities. In an earlier chapter I listed ways to enjoy creative solitude. It deepens and enriches you. You grow and become an interesting person, increasing the chances of successful socialization.

Your second priority should be to develop casual social relationships. This can be done during your day-to-day activities as well as at special social and recreational events. The goal is not intimate relationships, but to enlarge and stabilize your community. Community should come before intimacy.

Developing your personal community is a safe way to practice appropriate self-disclosure. It is a social skill that you will need when you are ready for intimate relationships. I practice self-disclosure at farm auctions.

The last auction I attended was up the street from my home. The farmer was selling and moving to Missouri. Seeking Alden out during a lull in the action, I told him how my father and I felt when we sold all our farm machinery and cattle at auction. My pet steer had gone for $141. Then I shared my feeling of loss with the farmer.

He became choked up as he responded to my self-disclosure. "A fellow never knows if he's doing the right thing or not," he said. "I felt like it was what I wanted to do, but now that it's happening, I don't know if it was the right decision. I think it probably is. At least I hope so. We'll see."

Then I told Alden how much I appreciated his being my neighbor. I let him know that I would miss him and his family. Complimenting him on having well-behaved children, I thanked him for his kindness. With my hand on his shoulder I wished him God's blessing.

Our time of self-disclosure was rewarding. I felt no loneliness as I opened myself to him and he to me.

As the drone of the auctioneer continued, I shuffled from one row of sale items to another, chatting with the men and women inspecting things. When I came to an item that brought back childhood memories, I shared them with a person nearby. Frequently they traded memories with me. I have come to view auctions as a type of therapy, a time to get in touch with my roots, and am learning to know more about myself, which I think is an excellent way to avoid loneliness.

I patronize a local copy shop in which I know all the employees. They know me as the minister who raids the candy dish. Also they know which candies I like best. When the dish gets low, they rummage through their supply to find my favorite. We have discussed our personal views on teenage dating, grandchildren, local politics, alcohol consumption, Bible versions, money-hungry TV evangelists, parenting, honesty, hard work, day care for small children, and a host of other topics. The last time I was in the shop, an employee told me about each of her children and I related how proud I was of my own grandchildren.

Every time I leave home, I am expanding my community. When I shop, I meet friends and feel a part of the place where I live.

Once you have a solid community in place, you have a basis for the development of intimate relationships. By intimate relationships I mean friendships that allow and welcome sharing at deeper, more personal levels. But it is something you can't rush. You can't force intimacy. Instead, it happens when you are content in your community. It is natural, not strained.

One evening I was putting the last-minute touches to the room where I hold my support groups. A man and a woman who had lost their spouses just a few months ago entered. It was the second time they had seen each other.

"I understand you are into antique cars," the man said.

"Yes." The woman sounded cautious.

"Well, you and I have a lot in common. I'm into antique tractors. I think we ought to get together. I'd really like to take you out to eat sometime so we can talk about our interests."

The silence was awkward. The woman busied herself with her coat and finally went to the counter where the snacks and drinks were placed. When she returned to the group, she chose a different seat.

After the session ended, a woman who knew the man well informed me that he was determined to date the woman. He would not take no for an answer. Lonely, he could not tolerate living without a female companion. Judging by what I saw, I don't think his plans will work. Putting the cart before the horse, he is in for disappointment, because he isn't willing to be content with himself and the process of building his community. His drivenness will lead him only to more loneliness.

For many years I listened to Dr. Lynn Weiss, a radio talk show counselor in Dallas, Texas. Many people asked her about remarriage after the loss of a spouse. Most of them expressed how lonely they were. She always urged them not to make a lifetime commitment for at least two years after the loss. She saw such quick marriages as a drive to eliminate loneliness.

Both parties must take plenty of time to determine that they are both mature. They need to know that any marital expectations they might have are realistic. And both should be sure their decision to remarry is rational instead of a rush of romantic passion. Do they both have a healthy self-image? Communication skills need to be in place, and they must discover if they have similar faith and values. If they have not determined these factors, they could easily be rushing into a lifetime commitment that will take them into a valley of loneliness deeper and darker than the one they already travel.

Dr. Laura Schlessinger repeatedly advises people who call her radio talk show to slow down and make decisions about relationships based on rational thinking instead of emotional reactions. She observes that too many people "interpret being alone as a major negative assessment of themselves and an annihilation of hope" *(How Could You Do That?* p. 108). Making rational decisions takes lots of courage.

Relationship decisions on the basis of feelings alone will get you into a heap of problems, one of which is loneliness. That's probably why Schlessinger says, "It's when you blend feelings with a major dose of courage, conscience, and rational thought that you connect to the most self-respectful aspects of your humanity" *(ibid.,* p. 142).

To make relationship decisions any other way will only lead to disaster. I see lonely adults violating their values for the sake of feeling good for one night, but leaving the pathway of their values only plummets them into the quagmire of guilt and more loneliness.

CONCENTRATE ON PERSONAL GROWTH

Personal growth enhances us and opens the doors to relationships with others, thus preventing chronic loneliness. If you are not growing, you become sterile and thus boring.

My wife discovered that when she took a job on an assembly line. For eight hours women stood at an assembly belt packing toy dishes. They gossiped and picked at each other, bragging about their cheap lifestyles. Lunchtime was a disaster for my wife, a woman who is constantly trying to develop her intellect. She had nothing in common with women who had no desire to better themselves. One week later she found a job that challenged her.

Talented people with broad interests are always rewarding friends. They can talk about a wide variety of topics and are eager to learn from others who know more than they do. In social settings such people have no trouble engaging in friendship development.

In addition to personal growth, a lonely person needs to learn the art of listening. One sure way to kill relationships is to dominate the conversation with topics of interest to you alone.

I was waiting for my wife to finish her eye doctor appointment. As I sat in the reception room, a young woman finished her business at the appointment desk. An older woman approached the desk, noticed the young woman, and proceeded to talk to her. At first the young woman appeared polite and friendly, but the scene changed.

The older woman proceeded to relate her life story. She told about her children, her mother's death, her brother's accident, her husband's Alzheimer's disease, and her loneliness. As she talked nonstop, I noticed the young woman walk to her chair and pick up her coat. With a polite nod she retreated from the doctor's office.

Personal growth and interest in many topics is fine, as long as you know how to listen and show interest in the other person. It's best to wait until your sharing can be part of a discussion already in progress. Your loneliness can grow by leaps and bounds when people avoid you or walk out on you.

Give People Breathing Room

Suffocating possessiveness of others is a foolproof way to drive them away, leaving you lonelier than before. Give people breathing room, and friendship will grow.

I was lucky when it came to college roommates. They all wanted the understanding that rooming together was fine, but possessing each other was out. I had my circle of friends and round of activities. They had theirs. Two of those roommates have continued to stay in touch with me. We have had rewarding social gatherings during the past 40 years. Our relaxed attitude about friendship has actually preserved the friendships.

Henri Nouwen has commented that "friendship and love cannot develop in the form of an anxious clinging to each other" (*Reaching Out*, p. 19). He believes that it is fear that causes a person to cling too closely, just as it is fear that causes too much distance. "Both prevent intimacy from developing"

(*Lifesigns*, p. 30). When the other person moves away to avoid suffocation, loneliness strikes.

STAY PUT

I've read the studies that show that mobility rates have remained relatively stable from 1800 to the present. Also I've read that loneliness caused by mobility is probably no more common now than it was a century ago, but that does not mean that the loneliness caused by mobility is not painful and destructive.

If I had it to do over again, I would move less. I hate to think of the thousands of dollars my denomination spent to move me 12 times in 39 years. That's an average of 3.25 years per place of residence and work. Our family experienced loneliness during those 39 years that took its toll. It doesn't matter how well we adjusted to the changes or how little we talked about being lonely. Loneliness still visited our home.

Some of the moves took place when our sons were adolescents. I saw them struggle with loneliness. When the home is new, the school is new, the community is new, and new friends have not yet materialized, life can be very empty for young people. Our sons felt that emptiness too many times.

One year after an accident killed our oldest, the hospital system where I worked as a chaplain decided to close the spiritual-care department as a cost-cutting measure. Having to find other employment, I took another chaplaincy position, which meant our family would move from Michigan to Texas. My wife and I flew to Texas to interview over the weekend. I still recall sitting in a motel room weeping, not knowing exactly why. I think it was a combination of losing our son and the loneliness of the involuntary move. The day we departed from Michigan with all our belongings in a truck, my wife wept halfway to Texas. You can't convince me that staying put isn't wise.

Sometimes I have scoffed at the provincial ways of my family in Pennsylvania. Most of them live within 50 miles of our birthplace. But more and more I am coming to see the value of their stability. Mobility has robbed our sons of knowing their cousins and aunts and uncles. My sister tells me about family reunions that I have not attended for decades.

Some of my family members have had to simplify their lifestyle and be content with less, but the dividends of being near family are looking more and more attractive to them. Being close to the favorite spots of childhood can create a sense of belonging. It can prevent existential loneliness. Faraway places don't hold a candle to the place you first called home.

I have met many ministers and their families. As I have presented seminars all over the United States and Canada, they have shared with me. Being separated from loved ones by hundreds and even thousands of miles has not done them any favors. All the research in the world cannot justify the kind of uprootedness that has created dreadful loneliness in entire families.

With envy I read about other ministers who have served God and church in the same location for decades. Why can't more of us stay put?

VIEW FRIENDSHIPS REALISTICALLY

During childhood and adolescence we sometimes believe that friends are friends forever. When they evaporate with the morning dew, we feel crushed and betrayed. Sooner or later we learn the difficult lesson that friendships are fleeting at that age.

The prettiest girl in my fifth-grade class was Sylvia. I liked her very much, and I think she liked me. Near Valentine's Day our teacher opened the red Valentine box and passed out the cards. I received two from Sylvia that year, but none the following year. Instead, Sylvia honored another boy with a large Valentine, bigger than any I had ever gotten from anyone in my life. That was a gigantic blow to my young heart. Now I think I understand.

When we are young, our interests change as we change. People who were like us in the seventh grade are different than we are in the tenth grade. We no longer feel close. When this happens we sometimes judge ourselves harshly, conclud-ing that there's something wrong with us when there really isn't. We are just different, and so are they. Although we feel lonely, it isn't because we are flawed human beings. If we could understand the nature of friendship in childhood and youth, perhaps we could be more realistic in our expectations of it. Very likely our loneliness would not be as difficult to work through.

I attended a church-operated high school in my senior year. Sitting across from me in Bible class was a young woman who appeared to be happy and friendly. My heart set on dating her, I practiced my request for more than a week. Finally the words came out in her presence. She smiled and said, "Larry, I'd really like to. Thank you for asking me, but I have other plans."

The first time wasn't so disappointing. I'd wait for two weeks and ask again. The second time she was a bit more apologetic. "Larry, I really feel terrible about turning you down, but I really am tied up." This time I looked at myself in the mirror and questioned myself. After all, I looked neat and clean. I had a nice smile. What was there about me that she didn't like?

Being the persistent fellow that I am, I tried a third time. Her response was apologetic and negative. Figuring that three strikes was out, I gave up.

At graduation time that pretty girl came to congratulate me, but she had still another message for me. "Larry, I have to tell you how sorry I am. I turned you down three times. Believe me, I have the highest regard for you. I hated to hurt your feelings, but I married someone during Christmas vacation. As you know, that is a violation of school rules. Because I had to keep it a secret, I couldn't tell you why I would not date you."

The experience taught me that it doesn't pay to flagellate yourself when friendships don't develop as you expect them to. There are too many unknown factors to make firm assumptions. Expect that some friendships are not forever and that others will never fly. Viewing friendships realistically will save you much loneliness.

Don't Tough It Out

When you have suffered a major loss, don't try to tough it out alone. Attend a good support group that addresses the gutsy issues of pain. Find one that gives you practical ways of walking through it. Use the services of a good counselor, a pastor, or a knowledgeable friend. Loneliness is a close companion of grief, so you'll want to grieve as soon and as intensely as you can. Postponing grief stretches it out over a longer time so that it takes a greater toll on you.

During my work in psychiatric units I have met patients undergoing treatment for all sorts of emotional problems. When I read their charts, I seldom found any mention of major losses, but when I developed their trust, they told me the rest of their story. Many of them had major losses 8, 10, 20, and even 40 years earlier. They had never received any support during their grief. Without support they tried to tough it out alone, but it wasn't working. As the years went by, they no longer attributed their emotional turmoil to the loss. During their intake interview they didn't mention the losses.

I still vividly remember a conversation I had with a psychiatrist. He met me in the hall and said, "Larry, what are you doing with Margaret?"

Although a bit fearful, I said, "Doctor, we are visiting every day. During the visits we are talking about the death of her husband 16 years ago. Why do you ask?"

"I'm just curious, Larry. She's been a patient several times in the past and doesn't seem to snap out of her problems, but since she has been chatting with you, I've seen vast improvements. Keep it up. I appreciate it."

Margaret is one of many who tried to manage loss without support. Invariably it leads to deep loneliness and emotional complications. We have a natural longing to lean on others when we are grieving, but others often tell us that we should be able to handle it. Western society discourages leaning. But I encourage it—encourage it because the apostle Paul told us to comfort one another with the comfort we ourselves have received from God. Scripture also advises us to bear one another's burdens. That sounds like leaning to me. So go ahead and lean. You won't lean forever. One day you'll be strong enough to be a shoulder for someone else.

DON'T BE AFRAID TO TOUCH

When I moved to Toledo, Ohio, a certain amount of loneliness accompanied the change in job and home. A young couple came to our little home on a Sabbath afternoon and invited us to a picnic. What a tonic for three people who still did not feel at home. A few years later the friends adopted a little boy. They were just beginning to enjoy their enlarged family when the mother had a recurrence of tuberculosis. Admitted to a TB sanatorium, she found herself separated from her husband and tiny baby boy. Month after month she was forced to look out of her window for a glimpse of her new boy. In spite of knitting and reading, she became desperately lonely. Depression followed.

One day her pastor visited her in the sanatorium. He never touched her, but stood five feet from the foot of her bed, chatted for a few minutes, prayed, and then left the room. Heading for a sink in the hall, he rolled up his sleeves and scrubbed his arms and hands. Watching it from her bed, she felt like an ugly leper who should have been screaming "Unclean, unclean." Her loneliness intensified.

When I heard about her hospitalization, I went to see her. Quickly I went to the head of her bed, grasped her hands in mine, and told her how sorry I was to hear of her illness and how glad I was for the chance to visit. Pulling up a chair, I listened until she ran out of energy. After praying with her, I left the hospital; minus the scrubbing.

The next time I saw her husband, he told me that my visit, particularly my willingness to touch her, had lifted her loneliness and sorrow. I had learned a valuable treatment for loneliness.

Since then I myself have had the touch of kindness and acceptance. I have felt loneliness lift with the soft touch of a caring person. My wife is an expert at this kind of touching. After

I had endured eight days of chills from malaria and the loneliness of hospitalization, her touch soothed me.

Lonely people should decide that they will not withdraw. They should be open to the touch of others and themselves take the opportunities to touch others who need a lift. Going to church is a good place to receive and give touch. Don't take handshakes for granted. We should value them as therapy for loneliness.

When I was a ministerial intern a young couple in my church had a baby who died at birth. They could not speak English. A pastor who spoke their language agreed to meet me and the father at the cemetery. We had the burial, but the mother was confined to bed. My wife and I went to the apartment to visit and bring them Communion. That lonely, sad mother knew what she needed. She reached up, put her arms around my wife, pulled her down onto the pillow with her, and hugged and cried. The bed shook with her sobbing. That touching and holding was the most valuable part of the visit. I saw the healing of touch before my eyes.

Loneliness cannot survive long with the touch of tenderness and love.

Avoid Addictive Lifestyles

Addictive lifestyles and addictive substances may help you to forget your loneliness for a brief time, but they cause you to focus on satisfying yourself. You withdraw from people, which only sinks you into more loneliness. Loving people may be there for you, but your addiction blinds you to their interest.

I have met too many addicted people in emergency rooms. When they were more sober, they told me of their loneliness and their failure to drown it with substances. Many have told me their stories of failure to eradicate loneliness with substances. I know it doesn't work.

Avoid the Loneliness Trap

The loneliness trap is the mistaken idea that we should be

totally self-sufficient and independent. Its inventors have tried to tell us that we are sick if we ever so slightly depend on others. As James Lynch puts it, "interpersonal freedom is the melody they play, and thousands march in step behind them. These pipers trap people because they make them feel guilty for even admitting that they are lonely; they insinuate that it is a sign of weakness to admit publicly that a person really needs someone else" (*The Broken Heart*, p. 207).

According to such gurus of independence, the song I sang in college about no man being an island, no man standing alone, is a recipe for sickness. But the philosophy of self-sufficiency flies in the face of the Creator's idea that it isn't good for us to live alone.

A certain amount of dependency is necessary to build a neighborhood. My neighbor told me not to buy a snow blower, because he has a blade for the front of his pickup truck. Another neighbor stopped by one day last fall to ask me to stop by for a visit when the weather is cold. He didn't want us getting lonely. A young man who lives a quarter mile up the road offered to let me use his harrow for my landscaping project. When we go on vacation, we call a neighbor to keep an eye on our house. The man next door saw me cutting a large strip of weeds with a scythe. He told me he would mow them with his father-in-law's brush hog. A neighbor gave me the key to his house. He and his wife go to Nevada every winter. A light blinks in a window when the temperature drops too low, and he wants me to check the furnace. Do I have sick neighbors because they are not totally self-sufficient and don't want me to be the same? Indeed not.

Never buy into this fallacy. It will lead you into a life of loneliness. We need each other—need to lean at times and other times allow others to lean on us. I'm not talking about taking unfair advantage of others, but rather about healthy interdependence that makes up a real community.

HAVE AN ACTIVE STATE OF MIND
One authority states that loneliness and despair are pas-

sive states of mind that we can overcome only by active states of mind, and advocates setting aside a time each day for contemplative exercise. You can use the time for spiritual meditation. Try asking yourself whether you showed kindness to anyone. Or figure out why you were unable to do so. Make plans to help another person. Such an approach supports the idea given to me by a teacher who told me that "it is easier to act your way into a new way of feeling than it is to feel your way into a new way of acting."

CHECK YOUR GAZE

Meeting an extremely lonely man who spent a year in therapy, I asked him what they had talked about in their sessions. He told me they had used the time combing through his childhood to find the source of his loneliness. What a waste.

Looking back at the past can cheat you out of life in the present and worsen your loneliness. The flip side of that is focusing on the future in hopes that your loneliness will end through no effort of your own. Either gaze will cement you into your loneliness. Our perception of what is happening in life can make a difference. My friend Terry proved that to me. He introduced me to selling Fuller Brush products. Terry went to homes with the thought in his mind that everybody liked Fuller brushes. Fully convinced of that, he met every householder with a big smile, a squirt of hand cream, and a free toothbrush. Seldom did he leave a home without an order. His gaze, his perception, made a difference.

Lonely people tend to rehearse the loneliness of the past, making it easy for them to believe they will always be lonely. They carry dirty laundry from days gone by in an overstuffed suitcase. That suitcase is so heavy that they can't walk into the present, let alone dream of a brighter future.

A lecturer at a convention I once attended said that you can starve to death in a full pantry if all you do is look at the floor. Gaze at your loneliness constantly and you can die of loneliness with possibilities of friendship and dialogue all around you. The direction of our gaze makes a difference.

Are There Solutions?

Work on Your Marriage

In an age of disposable relationships some married couples quickly decide to hang up their marriage as soon as they encounter problems. Yet with some hard work they could keep the marriage together and save themselves a mountain of loneliness. Divorce has its own set of loneliness producers. In many cases people could, if they worked at it, turn the marriage into a source of happiness. But that requires a decision to work hard. All good marriages are good because two people are working intensely to keep them that way.

Put Family First

Healthy families don't just happen. It takes time, energy, perseverance, patience, love, and commitment. And healthy families don't believe the lie that quality time, not quantity of time, is important. Happy families have both.

I'm convinced that giving family top priority prevents loneliness. Parents and children are much healthier when the family spends lots of time together. Sharing feelings of gratitude, joy, and sorrow with each other, they can be dreamers and visionaries. They can make important decisions and difficult decisions and test their values and grow together.

Our oldest son spent hours on the floor of my study. I usually had sermon notes taped to my wall as I typed my "masterpiece" for the worship hour, but that was secondary when my son stretched out on the floor. He needed to talk about what he wanted to do in life. It was a toss-up between an English major and a theology major. He ended up with both, but he didn't have to make that decision alone.

Our third son had so many interests and aptitudes that he struggled with his major in college. Our family drove to Palestine, Texas, to ride the old steam train there and to picnic at the end of the run. It was a good four-hour trip. I don't remember most of the details of the train ride, but I have a clear mental recording of what we said in the car. We spent most of our drive time discussing his lifework. Torn between teaching and preaching, he ended up doing both. As with his brother, he didn't have to make that decision by himself.

Decision-making can be a lonely task if you don't have the support of your family. Young people who live in a healthy family don't have to experience that loneliness. Families who are active tend to be less lonely. Vacationing together, doing household chores as a family, listening to favorite music, and helping neighbors provide time to learn and grow together.

Society tells us that we need material things to have a happy family, but their acquisition takes money. That means spending more time on the job and even holding down a second job to pay for them. Families end up separated because of their quest for things.

Families who are not lonely have learned to simplify life. They live with fewer material belongings so they can have more time together.

Our family looked forward to a week or two of camping each summer. No Airstream beauty behind an F-10 pickup. Just a borrowed tent and well-worn sleeping bags. When we pulled into a state park camping area, we tried to find a secluded camping spot away from those who brought the city with them. Rainy weather necessitated draping a big plastic sheet over the dozens of holes in the tent. We didn't have a dining tent, but eating camp food was delicious even when mosquitoes were giving their concert. Campfire smoke, a swimming hole, a few trails, and family worship in a cozy tent—what more could a family need to produce togetherness?

When we packed up that old Buick station wagon to go home, the weight in the back end made it look like a 747 with its nose wheels off the ground just before becoming totally airborne. Although we really didn't have much, we had each other. When our family gathers for holidays we still laugh and relive our times together. We believe that putting family first was worth it. That's what helped us to get through some of the lonely times.

Absentee parents produce children who are either clinging or aloof. Lacking self-confidence and trust, such children are prone to chronic loneliness. Putting family first can prevent this.

ESTABLISH A FAITH

Earlier in this book I discussed the role that alienation from God plays in loneliness. Tied to that alienation is alienation from others, self, and nature. Establishing a faith, then, is the place to begin if you are to break the grip of loneliness.

Unfortunately, faith has an unpleasant ring, because it is so often tied to religion. Religion in America has put a sour taste in the mouths of many, thanks to the big business approach so often seen on TV and in the junk mail. More and more "ministries" sprout up, and every one of them is trying to reach into the checkbook. Even within a given denomination the programs are constantly mushrooming. All of them advertise themselves as the solution to some serious problem. The calls for money and the scandal within various religious communities have caused people to program religious telecasts into their emotional V-chips.

When I suggest that you establish a faith, I am recommending that you sit down with your Bible regularly. Before you open it, quietly ask God to reveal Himself to you as you read. That's what the Bible is all about—God attempting to communicate with us. Don't form hasty conclusions. Read extensively and prayerfully, and you will gradually come to understand that our sovereign God sustains the universe and is involved in the daily affairs of His creatures. You will discover that God has a master plan to restore His image fully in us.

As you come in contact with God in Scripture and in your simple prayers and quiet meditation, you will find a gradually growing trust. You will come to believe that God has a purpose for your life. Every day will become another chance to see that purpose unfold. Meaning and the lessening of loneliness will accompany that unfolding.

Reading many research reports on loneliness has taught me that quite a few researchers discovered that people with a faith were less likely to be lonely.

When I began to mature in my own personal faith, I found that I became less self-focused. I wanted to treat other people the way God did me. With less self-focus came a decrease in bouts of loneliness. And it happened to me when I was an adolescent, a time when loneliness is at its peak.

I was baptized into the church when I was 12. At that time we lived on an old plantation farm in southern Pennsylvania. A neighbor, a single parent with three children, was lighting her cookstove one day. She poured what she thought was kerosene on the smoldering fire, but it was gasoline. The explosion seriously burned her and extensively damaged her house. While she was in the hospital, a group of neighbors remodeled her house and furnished it completely. I was intensely interested in this project. Forgetting about my own concerns, I found great happiness in working for that little family. Renovating their home brought me close to neighbors my own age as well as older people. We laughed together, prayed together, ate together, and worked together. My faith gave me a genuine interest in that family, and the result was a personal satisfaction.

Since then I have found that when my personal faith wanes, I become more self-focused and more prone to loneliness.

Once you have a faith relationship with God, you can look around for a faith community that supports your faith and nurtures you. You also need a faith community that will give you the opportunity to serve others.

Examine Your Spaces

I've discovered that many lonely people operate at breakneck speed. They constantly try to squeeze two days into one, leaving little time for creative solitude and the development of relationships.

Why not examine the spaces in which you live? You have a work space, a home space, a community space, a recreation space, a school space, and an inner space (your attitudes and perspectives on life). You can add others, I'm sure.

Any of your spaces can become sick if you pour an enormous amount of energy into one of them but receive few rewards, little reverse flow of energy. When you get no affirmation, no appreciation, no incentives for personal growth, no control over the amount of energy spent, and no sense of fulfillment, the space you are examining is sick. Living in a sick space can wear you out physically, emotionally, and spiritually. It can make you lonely.

Instead of complaining about how dragged out and lonely you are, take charge of your spaces. You can change them, make them healthy.

If you discover a sick space, try to think of ways to make that space healthy. I'll give you an example.

One time I presented a stress management seminar for the Florist Association of Dallas/Fort Worth. The president of a large floristry business stopped me on my way to the parking lot. "Larry, you made my day. I have spent lots of money over the past two years training my vice president to take over the business when I retire. Today he told me he wants out. I'm going crazy. But hearing you tonight gives me hope. Can we come visit you in the next few days?"

The two men arrived at my office two days later. It was clear that their work space was extremely sick. The vice president had to exit that space to preserve his sanity.

"How often do you sweep the floor in your flower shop?" I asked.

"What's that have to do with anything?" the president protested.

"Don't argue. Just answer my questions."

"Once a day," he replied.

"Sweep it four times during the workday. It is aggravating stepping on trash all day."

Then I looked at the younger man and asked, "When you talk business, where and how do you do it?"

"In the shop. Loudly," he responded.

"Gentlemen," I advised, "discuss business away from the shop and speak in a civil tone of voice."

Again I looked at the vice president. "What does your organizational flowchart look like?"

He described a chart with the president at the top and the vice president on the same level with the managers of design, production, and delivery. Telling them to put the vice president below the president and above the three managers, I urged them to meet with all employees and review the new flowchart.

"When you make a corsage, do you have to leave your stool to get flowers and wires and ribbons?" I questioned.

"Well, of course," the president answered.

"Organize your work area so that you can make a corsage without getting off the stool. That's all I have to offer when it comes to changing your work space. Give it a try. If you need further help, get back to me." I shook their hands and bid them a good day.

Two weeks later a dazzling bouquet arrived at my office. The attached card read "Thanks, Larry. We're back on track." Both the president and the vice president had signed it.

Once you determine that you can change a sick space, decide how and when you will do it. Put the most workable options into operation at once.

Some spaces may be temporarily sick. In that event you will need to cut back the energy you spend in other spaces until the sick one improves. You have only so much energy. Conserve it. Use it wisely.

If you discover that you can't change a sick space, you need to determine if your attitudes about the space are healthy. Try changing your perspectives on the situation. If that doesn't work, you'll need to exit that space. Decide when and how you can do that. Put your decisions into operation as soon as appropriate.

Remember the overstuffed suitcase I talked about? Restructuring your spaces is the way to unpack that suitcase and make it easier to carry. Instead of rushing at a mad pace, you'll have time for yourself and for others. And you'll have time to strengthen your relationship with God.

By the way, all you need is one sick space. It won't be long until it has infected all the spaces you live in. It's like the old one-rotten-apple-in-the-barrel saying. Don't waste any time. Cure those sick spaces. You'll find that it helps with the loneliness problem.

Are There Solutions?

Balance Your Life

Lonely people are usually out of balance. If they could strike a balance between work, relationships, time alone, and time with God, they would not have as much loneliness. But that takes discipline and patience and requires adjusting priorities.

Another part of balance is good nutrition. The food we eat affects our moods, and what we don't eat can do the same. I'm especially thinking about people who never have breakfast. Sensible eating habits and excellent nutrition will definitely improve the loneliness problem.

Rest and relaxation, along with adequate exercise, figure into the balance equation. It doesn't require a roomful of exercise equipment, however. A good pair of walking shoes will do the trick. Find a good relaxation technique that isn't loaded with Eastern religious exercises. Regulate your schedule to get eight or nine hours of sleep each night. The sense of well-being from these three activities will reduce your episodes with loneliness.

The last part of balance is taking care of your mind. Read books and magazines that are uplifting, free of violence and eroticism, and true to reality. Avoid most TV shows and movies. Determine that you will be in charge of what goes into your mind. The media presents an unrealistic view of happiness in life. Watching and listening to such material can cause you to set some unrealistic expectations from your relationships.

In the psychiatric units where I worked, I constantly observed patients glued to the TV during soap opera time. Many of the patients were very lonely for various reasons. The soap operas only added to their dissatisfaction with life. After I presented my thoughts on the matter to the staff, they decided to limit patient TV viewing. They closed the TV room during soap opera time.

Balancing life is a matter of guarding the avenues to the soul. It is focusing the mind on that which is true, good, honorable, peaceable, and encouraging. Such balance leads to less loneliness.

Push the Delete Button on Competition

Once I attended a large evangelism conference in New York. A church leader brought one evangelist after another to the podium and awarded them a plaque for having baptized 100 or more people in the previous year. I knew I'd never receive an award, because I was a young upstart who was lucky to pull a sermon together every week, let alone organize large public evangelistic crusades. Out of boredom I meandered through the hotel. As I entered the third-floor lounge, I noticed a colleague seated in a darkened corner. He was alone. As I greeted him I noticed that he had been weeping. Conversing with him, I learned that he felt separated from his colleagues. The competitive nature of the conference had created a deep loneliness.

Here was a man who had many battle scars. A peacemaker who accepted many difficult assignments and soothed many volatile feelings that were splitting congregations, he was a thorough scholar who guided many neophyte pastors. In controversial meetings he could stand up and calm the storm, yet this conference made him feel like a failure.

Even though he was about to retire and I was just beginning, I tried to tell my friend that he was a success. Counseling him to avoid the competitive rat race and refuse to get caught up in the nonsense of comparing himself with others, I asked him to celebrate his uniqueness.

You can drive yourself to loneliness by allowing the competitive schemes of others to manipulate you. If you want to compete, compete with yourself in the area of personal growth as long as your goals are realistic.

Too much of our materialistic society relies on competition to make a profit or to gain a great reputation. People who cherish peace of mind must combat this. It is vital to good mental health.

Reading the works of Paul Tournier drove this point home to me. I had never considered the role that competition plays in loneliness until I read his books. I would recommend this author. His writings are classics. Reading them may deliver you from the tyranny of competition as it did me.

ARE THERE SOLUTIONS?

CHALLENGE YOUR CULTURE

One time I spent a week in Korea lecturing on grief counseling. A young pastor explained to me that my method of encouraging people to share their feelings of sorrow would not work in the Korean culture. Telling him that while rituals differ in various countries, pain is still pain, no matter your nationality, I challenged him to confront his culture. If a practice is not healthy, try to change it. He smiled politely and departed.

During the week the pastors worked in the mornings and attended classes the rest of the day. On the third day of the session that young pastor was eager to share something with me. "Larry, I did what you told me to do. This morning I visited a member who lost her husband two years ago. Many times she had tried to tell me of her sadness, but I always changed the subject. This morning I encouraged her to talk. She talked and cried for two hours, and I listened just like you told me. When she was all finished, she told me she was so full of joy about being able to share herself. She wanted to thank me by giving me lunch."

Every culture clings to ways that are not healthy. People allow themselves to be controlled by attitudes and expectations that create and perpetuate loneliness. If we are to break the hold that loneliness has on us, we must confront our culture, must stop following like dumb sheep. We can use many of the suggestions I have listed, but confronting societal trends that produce loneliness is the biggest step we can take toward solving the loneliness problem.

Carpooling illustrates how difficult it is to break practices that promote loneliness. Large cities have pushed carpooling for years. They have set aside special express lanes for carpoolers and built secure parking lots where people can meet to complete their drive to work. Ads on radio and TV have targeted eliminating congestion and pollution. But it has been an uphill battle. People still sit in bumper-to-bumper traffic, alone in their poison-spewing cars. Think of the friendships that could develop if they carpooled or rode the bus.

Church architecture is another cultural hang-up that fosters loneliness. It fastens pews to the floor in choo-choo train fashion. Worshipers are spectators. When the show is over, the ushers dismiss by rows, lest the aisles become congested with people. The people file out and go to their cars without using the opportunity for fellowship.

A friend of mine nearly had his congregation tar and feather him back during the hippie era when he unbolted the pews of a large city church. He arranged them so that people faced each other instead of gazing at the backs of heads. Young people heard about the church and gladly sat in the re-arranged pews, much to the dismay of the charter members.

Look around you. Examine the cultural practices that need challenging. Ask questions. Help to change the unhealthy traditions. You may break the cords of loneliness in your own life and open the doors of hope for others.

CHAPTER ELEVEN

Recipe or Process?

From the time I was big enough to stand on a kitchen chair, I watched my mother make Pennsylvania Dutch potpie. Unfortunately, I couldn't tell you how she created the base for the dish, because my main interest was the dough.

Mother dumped flour, shortening, a few eggs, and I think a little salt into her huge mixing bowl. She stirred it with her hands until a big ball of soft dough lay on the bottom of the bowl. Then she sprinkled flour on the oilcloth-covered table and dumped the dough on top of it. A few sprinkles of flour on top of the dough, and Mother was ready for the rolling pin. After rolling the dough until it was halfway across the table, she cut strips one inch wide and four inches long with a knife. Now the fun began.

She stacked the strips on her open hand. When her hand was full, she laid the strips on her arm all the way to her elbow. Going to the boiling kettle, one by one she dropped the strips into the delicious-smelling base. When the strips were all in the kettle, she put the lid on and moved the kettle to the cooler side of the old cookstove.

By suppertime that kettle was the center of attention for two parents and eight children. We argued about who would get the scrapings at the bottom of the kettle. I mean, potpie was an integral part of home.

When I married, I frequently told Roberta about Pennsylvania Dutch potpie. She soon tired of my not-too-subtle remarks. At Thanksgiving we visited my parents. Roberta asked my mother for the recipe. My mother had a strange look on her face, because she hadn't used a potpie recipe for decades. What do you mean, a recipe? After some coaxing, Roberta convinced my mother to tell her how she made potpie as my wife attempted to write it down. It was a long ordeal, because my mother had an uncanny sense of what ingredients and what quantities went into the amazing dish and had always followed that instead of using preset amounts. Now she did some wild guessing about teaspoons, tablespoons, and cups, but in the end Roberta had the "recipe" neatly arranged on her paper.

Back in Washington, D.C., my wife set about to satisfy my yen for potpie, but try as she might, she never produced the delicacy I ate as a child. I'm sure that my favorite potpie resulted partly because of Mother's inherent sense of proportions and flavors, but more than likely because of my ravenous childhood appetite and the entire home environment. You see, my mother's Pennsylvania Dutch potpie was a process, not a dish or a recipe.

When I first became interested in the topic of loneliness, I was looking for a recipe, a clear-cut definition of what it is. But quickly I discovered that loneliness has many dimensions, many ingredients, many causes. For each person loneliness is a process. The roots may go back to genetic makeup. Certainly they trace back to childhood. Societal expectations and attitudes figure in to the recipe. How much of this and that makes for loneliness is really up for grabs. The researchers grapple with surveys and tests, but they end up recommending more research. After examining my own loneliness and that of others, I have concluded that for each one of us loneliness is a process, not a recipe.

When I searched for remedies, I came to the same conclusion. There are no precise formulas, methods, serums, pills, or treatments to cure it. No secret recipe for developing life-enriching relationships or for achieving the elixir of life known as dialogue.

By conversing with lonely people, reading about loneliness, and examining my own personal loneliness, I have come up with many ingredients that could be used. No specific recipe has emerged, because living with loneliness is a process. Each person's process will be different, but those processes can still be effective. They can lead to a satisfying and joyful life.

A volunteer in my bereavement support group has struggled with chronic loneliness. She turned to religion, thinking she'd find answers there. Church people told her that loneliness would disappear if she turned her life over to God. They gave her the clear impression that it is not a process. One day you are a lonely sinner. The next day you are free of crippling loneliness.

Although she gave her life to God, the chronic loneliness did not vanish overnight. Perplexed at first, she thought that perhaps she didn't understand what her religious friends had said. She spoke about it to some Christians in the church. They assured her that the loneliness should have vanished. Then her perplexity turned to guilt.

Maybe I haven't really given my life to God, she thought. *Maybe I haven't studied the Bible enough. Is it possible that I didn't pray hard enough? Do you suppose I need to start doing more for God? Perhaps God is punishing me for the bad things I did before I came to Him.*

Her struggles continued for months until her loneliness and discouragement turned into depression. When her Christian friends heard about her depression, they told her that good Christians don't get depressed. That sent her into a deeper depression. The pain was so intense that she would sit at a traffic light and contemplate pulling out in front of an 18-wheeler. That's when she decided to go for help.

Her counselor was very wise. His understanding of loneliness and depression helped him to put things in perspective for her. He guided her in discovering the causes of her loneliness and depression. Encouraging her in her new relationship with God, he also told her that eliminating the chronic loneliness was going to be a process in which God would be assisting her. When she understood that there was no recipe to eliminate loneliness instantly, she was more at peace.

Three years have passed since that encounter. She has occasional transient loneliness, but the chronic loneliness has gone. Enjoying her family, she is finding fulfillment as a volunteer.

I told my volunteer friend that handling loneliness was a process for Jesus, too. He felt every bump in the road through the valley of loneliness. The traditions of His own people ambushed Him. Rejection faced Him every day. Others brought up His past and hurled it in His face. People put Him down because of His Nazareth home, His lowly trade, His parentage, and His education. They questioned His motives. In the Garden of Gethsemane He nearly died of loneliness. His closest friends deserted Him. Falsely accused, He died a death He did not deserve. Jesus knew the bumps in the road and understands those in our own valleys of loneliness.

As I study Jesus' life, I realize that He knew how to get through the valley of loneliness. That has been the delight of my study. He challenged the traditions of His culture, confronted those who would plant negative images in His mind. Gladly He mingled with many types of people. Other-focused and kingdom-focused, He daily performed healing acts. An intimacy giver, not only an intimacy taker, He communed with the Father and trusted the Father's purpose for him. Willing to express both His sorrow and His joy, He took every opportunity to have dialogue with individuals. His compassion for the crowds was obvious. The long hours in the carpentry shop provided creative solitude and personal development. Jesus came to earth with a goal, and He achieved that goal. He had close communion with nature. That's why He used nature lessons in His teaching. Low self-esteem was not a problem. He knew where He came from and where He was going and was always a man of action with a purpose.

When I contemplate Jesus' journey through the valley of

loneliness, I am convinced that He can help you and me make the journey also. By His strength we will soon enjoy the land where there exists no valley of loneliness.

As we walk through our valley, we must not travel alone. God created us to have fellowship with God and with our fellow voyagers. We must not heed the philosophies that advocate self-sufficiency and independence, nor believe those who would make every act of dependence a sickness. The practices of a competitive society that isolate us from others must be confronted and shunned. Above all, we must decide that we will not allow loneliness to take charge of our life. Each of us must take control of loneliness.

I think I have found the key to controlling my loneliness: deciding to help alleviate loneliness in the heart of my sister and my brother. As I accompany them on their journey through the valley of loneliness, I myself grow stronger. I have more endurance. Together we ascend to the heights of joy. When I become the keeper of my sister and my brother, I discover that I have kept myself from sinking into the quicksand of loneliness.

It is my prayer that sharing these pages with you will make the journey easier for both of us.

BIBLIOGRAPHY

Benson, Herbert. *Timeless Healing.* New York: Scribner, 1996.

Brennan, Tim, and N. Auslander. *Adolescent Loneliness.* Prepared for the National Institute of Mental Health, Behavorial Research Institute, 1979.

Carter, Les, Paul D. Meier, and Frank B. Minirth. *Why Be Lonely?* Grand Rapids: Baker Book House, 1982.

Ditzen, Lowell Russell. *You Are Never Alone.* New York: Henry Holt and Co., 1956.

Durham, Charles. *When You Are Feeling Lonely.* Downers Grove, Ill.: InterVarsity Press, 1984.

Fisher, Bruce. *Rebuilding.* San Luis Obispo, Calif.: Impact Publishers, 1981.

Flanders, James P. "A General Systems Approach to Loneliness," in Letitia Peplau and Daniel Perlman, eds. *Loneliness: A Sourcebook of Current Theory, Research, and Therapy.* New York: John Wiley and Sons, 1982.

Gonzalez-Balado, Jose Luis, ed. *Mother Teresa: In My Own Words.* Liguori, Mo.: Liguori Publications, 1996.

Gordon, Suzanne. *Lonely in America.* New York: Simon and Schuster, 1976.

Hart, Archibald D. *Children and Divorce.* Waco, Tex.: Word Books, 1982.

Hulme, William E. *Creative Loneliness.* Minneapolis: Augsburg Publishing House, 1977.

Irwin, James B. *To Rule the Night.* Philadelphia: A. J. Holman, 1973.

Kaiser, Robert Blair. "The Way of the Journal," *Psychology Today*, March 1981.

Kidner, Derek. *Genesis.* Downers Grove, Ill.: Inter-Varsity Press, 1967.

Kiley, Dan. *Living Together, Feeling Alone.* New York: Prentice Hall Press, 1989.

Lynch, James J. *The Broken Heart—The Medical Consequences of Loneliness.* New York: Basic Books, 1977.

———. *The Language of the Heart.* New York: Basic Books, 1985.

Myers, David G. *The Pursuit of Happiness.* New York: Avon Books, 1992.

Natale, Samuel M. *Loneliness and Spiritual Growth.* Birmingham, Ala.: Religious Education Press, 1986.

Nouwen, Henri J. M. *Intimacy.* Notre Dame, Ind.: Fides/Claretian, 1969.

——— and Walter J. Gaffney. *Aging.* New York: Doubleday and Co., 1976.

———. *Letters to Marc About Jesus.* San Francisco: Harper and Row, 1988.

———. *Lifesigns.* New York: Doubleday and Co., 1986.

———. *Out of Solitude.* Notre Dame, Ind.: Ave Maria Press, 1984.

———. *Reaching Out.* New York: Doubleday and Co., 1975.

———. *The Wounded Healer.* New York: Doubleday, 1972.

Oates, Wayne E. *Nurturing Silence in a Noisy Heart.* New York: Doubleday and Co., 1979.

———. *The Psychology of Religion.* Waco, Tex.: Word Books, 1973.

Peplau, Letitia Anne, and Daniel Perlman, eds. *Loneliness—A Sourcebook of Current Theory, Research, and Therapy.* New York: John Wiley and Sons, 1982.

Rubenstein, Carin, and Phillip Shaver. *In Search of Intimacy.* New York: Delacorte Press, 1982.

Seamands, David A. *If Only.* Wheaton, Ill.: Victor Books, 1995.

Schlessinger, Laura. *How Could You Do That?* New York: Harper-Collins Publishers, 1996.

Stewart, Charles William. *The Minister as Family Counselor.* Nashville: Abingdon, 1979.

Tournier, Paul. *Escape From Loneliness.* Philadelphia: Westminster Press, 1967.

White, John. *Putting the Soul Back in Psychology.* Downers Grove, Ill.: Intervarsity Press, 1987.

APPENDEXES

Appendix A

A MODEL OF LONELINESS SITUATIONS

Loss of Community—
    Business acquaintances
    Church family
    Neighbors
    Delivery persons (UPS, etc.)
    Service acquaintances
    School

Loss of Intimacy—
    Social intimacy
    Physical intimacy
    Emotional intimacy
    Aesthetic intimacy
    Intellectual intimacy
    Sexual intimacy
        via
        immediate family
        extended family
        confidant
        spouse
High expectations and low reality

RESULTS

Basic Human Needs Unmet—
- Love (giving and receiving)
- Belonging
- Touch of tenderness
- Security
- Purpose/role
- Creativity
- Sense of accomplishment
- Acceptance
- Recognition

HENCE—LONELINESS

Appendix B

A MODEL OF LONELINESS—SITUATIONS

Alienation from God
Alienation from self
Alienation from others
Alienation from nature

RESULTS

Lack of identity
Lack of purpose/role
Low self-esteem
Insufficient human contacts
No sense of belonging to a larger scheme
Lack of acceptance
Insecurity
Lack of intimacy
Lack of community

HENCE—LONELINESS